MEMORIES
NEWCASTLE
UPON TYNE

D1632589

NEWCASTLE CHRONICLE
& JOURNAL LTD

INCLUDING PHOTOGRAPHS FROM THE LIBRARY OF
THE NEWCASTLE CHRONICLE AND JOURNAL LIMITED

TRUE NORTH BOOKS
DEAN CLOUGH
HALIFAX
WEST YORKSHIRE
HX3 5AX
TEL 01422 344344

THE PUBLISHERS WOULD LIKE TO THANK THE
FOLLOWING COMPANIES FOR SUPPORTING THE
PRODUCTION OF THIS BOOK

MAIN SPONSOR
NORTHERN ELECTRIC PLC

THOMAS BATY LIMITED

BEMCO LIMITED

THE DAVY ROLL COMPANY

ELDON SQUARE SHOPPING CENTRE

GRAINGER TRUST PLC

R MANNERS & SON LIMITED

NESTLÉ UK LIMITED

NEWCASTLE COLLEGE

NORTH BRITISH TAPES LIMITED

NORTHUMBRIAN WATER

THOMAS OWEN & SONS LIMITED

JOHN PORTER LIMITED

THE PORT OF TYNE AUTHORITY

THOMAS POTTER (NEWCASTLE) LIMITED

JAMES ROSS & SON LIMITED

STEPHENSON CLARKE SHIPPING LIMITED

FH THOMPSON & SONS LIMITED

E & F TURNBULL LIMITED

ACKNOWLEDGMENTS

THE PUBLISHERS WOULD LIKE TO THANK THE FOLLOWING COMPANIES FOR THEIR HELP IN MAKING
PHOTOGRAPHS AVAILABLE FOR THIS BOOK

NEWCASTLE CHRONICLE AND JOURNAL LTD
THE WARD PHILIPSON GROUP
BEAMISH MUSEUM.

Photographs with the letters NC&J are the copyright of Newcastle Chronicle & Journal Ltd. To order copies of these prints, please telephone Newcastle Chronicle & Journal on 0191 201 6001 and ask for a photosales order form.
Photographs with the letters WP are the copyright of the Ward Philipson Group. Copies of these images can be obtained by phoning 0191 2327281.

Introduction

Welcome to *Memories of Newcastle*, a look back on some of the places, events and people in the city which have shaped the lives of local people over a period of around half a century. The following pages are brought to life by a selection of images from the not-too-distant past, chosen according to their ability to rekindle memories of days gone by and show how people used to shop, work and play in the area they grew up. Modern image reproduction techniques have enabled us to present these pictures in a way rarely seen before, and the lively design and informative text is meant to bring these superb images to life.

One of Newcastle's most famous landmarks, the Tyne Bridge, completed in 1928

The chosen period is one which contains events generally within the memory of a large number of people in Newcastle - this is not a book about crinolines or bowler-hats! Neither is *Memories of Newcastle* a work of local history in the normal sense of the term. It has far more to do with entertainment than serious study, but we hope you will agree it is none the worse for that. It is hoped that the following pages will prompt readers own memories of Newcastle from days gone by - and we are always delighted to hear from people who can add to the information contained in the captions so that we can enhance future editions of the book.

Many local companies and organisations have allowed us to study their archives and include their history here - and fascinating reading it makes too! The present-day guardians of the firms concerned are proud of their products, the achievements of their people and the hard work of their forefathers whose efforts created these long established organisations. We are pleased to make it possible for them to share their history with a wider audience.

When we began compiling *Memories of Newcastle* we anticipated that the task would be a pleasurable one, but our expectations were greatly surpassed. There is a growing appetite for all things 'nostalgic' and we are pleased that this book will swell the number of images and associated information available to the growing number of enthusiasts. Our thanks go to the staff of *Newcastle Chronicle and Journal Ltd and Ward Philipson Group* for supplying many of the excellent photographs and for their enthusiastic encouragement.

There is much talk in modern times about the regeneration of the local economy, the influx of new industries and the challenge of attracting new enterprise from other regions to Tyneside. And quite right too. We could, however, make the mistake of thinking that the changes are all happening *now,* but the reality is that there have always been major developments going on in the city. 'Change' is relentless and the photographs on the pages in the book serve to remind us of some of them.

Memories of Newcastle has been a pleasure to compile, we sincerely hope you enjoy reading it.

Happy memories!

Mark Smith and Phil Holland
Publishers

© TRUE NORTH HOLDINGS
ISBN 1 900 463 81 4

CONTENTS

Events and occasions

NC & J

The atmosphere of central Newcastle in the early 1950s is captured magnificently by this photograph. The picture was one of a series taken to record the city-centre decorations displayed to celebrate the 1953 coronation. The large, dark-coloured *Browns* furniture store is shown on the right and the distinctive dome of the Central Exchange (built between 1836 and 1838, and rebuilt at the turn of the twentieth century after a devastating fire) can be seen beyond it. The building stands at the corner of Grainger Street and Market Street on a triangular site. In the distance it is just possible to see Grey's Monument, the tribute to Earl Grey which has stood on this spot since 1838.

NC & J

Above: The vessel *Campania* moored beside the Tyne in a photograph from June 1951. The ship's deck was fitted out with a broad platform above her striking white hull, and all had been decorated with flags and bunting to make a fitting home for the mobile exhibition. The Festival of Britain itself was, of course, already taking place on the South Bank of the Thames in London, having been opened a month earlier. The purpose of the exhibition was to lift people out of the post war gloom and foster a spirit of optimism and enterprise which might also assist efforts to kick-start the economy.

Left: A riveter works away as if unaware of the presence of King George and Queen Elizabeth. The engineer was part of a team repairing a ship at a North Shields yard. The picture was taken when the royal couple toured the area in June 1941 and shows the party of V.I.P.s, including the Mayor of Tynemouth and Councillor Anderson. Her Majesty was, characteristically, on top form and doing what she has always done best - putting everyone at their ease with her totally open and relaxed manner.

Top: During the Second World War a key role was played by King George VI and Queen Elizabeth. The royal couple toured the country relentlessly, visiting the sites of the worst bomb damage and motivating the workers involved with the production of all kinds of equipment needed for the war effort. This picture shows men working at Smith's Dock at North Shields. It was taken on June 19th 1941.

NC & J

Above: Beneath this tightly packed group of people were two flat-backed lorries, hastily converted into temporary grandstands from which the excited crowd could watch the local Victory Parade procession in Newcastle. Similar parades were taking place the length and breadth of the country involving virtually every 'service' which had played a part in the war - from the Army, Navy and Airforce to Local Defence Volunteers, youth organisations, church groups and medical care organisations. Of course, the celebrations were tinged with sadness as most people had experienced the loss of at least one person they knew or loved, but overall the atmosphere was one of joy and relief at the realisation that the enemy had at last been beaten, and everyone hoped that life would soon return to normal.

"Victory Parades took place the length and breadth of the country"

Right: Newcastle United's win in the 1952 F.A. Cup Final was, as you would expect, the signal for tremendous celebrations throughout the region. The team had just beaten Arsenal by one goal to nil in a lack-lustre match at Wembley. The Arsenal team had lost their defender Wally Barnes after an injury (from which he never recovered sufficiently to play soccer again) and struggled on valiantly with ten men for more than an hour. Even Milburn had a quiet game and it was left to George Robledo to head in the winner with just five minutes to go. The old offices of the *Newcastle Chronicle and Journal Ltd.* can be seen behind the statue of George Stephenson, inventor of the Geordie safety lamp for miners and father of Robert Stephenson. Dozens of members of staff from the various offices can be seen perched precariously on the window ledges of the buildings on the route of the procession, as they were throughout the whole of the city centre.

You would have to travel a long way to see a better display of coronation decorations than these along Grey Street. The centrepiece of this photograph is the single-decker coronation bus with a similarly-decorated double-decker version following close behind. They succeeded in turning heads wherever they went in the city. On the left the Royal Turk's Head had entered into the spirit of the occasion with an impressive display of its own. The property no longer acts as a hotel and was altered in 1991 along with some of the other properties on the block. In the distance, on the right, is the magnificent Theatre Royal. It dates from 1836 though it has been extensively restored on at least two occasions since then. It remains one of the most impressive buildings in Newcastle.

Above: The whole of Britain was in party mood for the coronation of Queen Elizabeth in June 1953, but preparation for the festivities began long before then. Throughout the country innovative ways of celebrating the event were embarked upon and virtually anything that stood still long enough to be decorated drew the attention of various coronation celebrations committees. This splendid effort was provided by Newcastle City Council. The *Coronation Bus* was as bright as a new pin when inspected by the Lord Mayor of Newcastle, Alderman William McKeag in May 1953 at the Byker Transport Depot.

Top: 'Long Live Our Queen' proclaimed the message on the front of this trolley bus. It was lavishly decorated in *the best possible taste* for the coronation of Britain's young queen in 1953. The picture was taken to support a story in the *Evening Chronicle* in May 1953 which described how the vehicle was being used on the Pier Head route in South Shields. The authorities were proud that no extra charge was being made on passengers on the route despite the privilege of riding on such a prestigious vehicle!

NC & J

NC & J

Above: It would be hard to imagine many youngsters of today getting as involved in cleaning in their street - to the extent of white washing the walls and scouring the cobblestones as these children did in June 1953. Yet the whole of the country was gripped by royal fever at the time of the coronation of Her Majesty Queen Elizabeth II - and typically Newcastle folk were not to be outdone or out-decorated by anyone. In London, despite the dreary weather, thousands of people packed the route on which their new monarch would travel to Westminster Abbey. It was said that 30,000 of them had camped overnight in the Mall to ensure that they would get a good view of the event. Use of balconies overlooking the route had been hired by people for up to £3,500 a time - a staggering amount of money in the 1950s. The coronation marked another point in social history, as the value of television sets became appreciated by ordinary people throughout the land. An estimated two and a half million sets were in place around the country with friends relatives and neighbours packed in front of them to watch the national spectacle.

Left: It was all hands on deck for the residents of this Newcastle street during the preparations for the coronation of 1953. People young and old rallied round to clean up the streets and put up displays of bunting, flags and even portraits of Her Majesty in preparation for the big day.
On the day of the coronation itself hundreds of street parties were held throughout the city. It was a day of great celebrations that would be remembered by the people of Tyneside for the rest of their lives.

NC & J

Above: The task of erecting yard after yard of red, white and blue bunting was taken very seriously by the residents of this street. The occasion was the coronation of Her Majesty Queen Elizabeth in 1953. Someone had had the idea of getting the children in the neighbourhood to hold the bunting off the ground while the man on the right carefully fixed it in a zig-zag pattern throughout the length of the street. A delightfully nostalgic picture from around half a century ago.

Right: In an age when most people are more familiar with the characters on Coronation Street than they are with their own neighbours, it is heart-warming to look back on a time when the words 'community spirit' had a very real meaning. This scene shows friends and neighbours on Pine Street working together to decorate their street for the 1953 coronation. It took four people to cling on to the ladder while a middle-aged gent carefully arranged flags around a portrait of the new monarch which was positioned above portraits of the Duke of Edinburgh, the young Prince Charles and the even younger Princess Anne.

NC & J

Who could fail to be impressed by the imposing, yet dignified twin towers of Newcastle's Co-operative building, especially when bedecked with all manner of elaborate decorations for the 1953 coronation? This stirring sight was recorded in May 1953 and features around a dozen delightful motor vehicles from the time which evoke feelings of nostalgia in anyone who experienced a ride in one of them during this period. The centre piece of the photograph is the magnificent Co-operative building itself which dominates the Newgate Street area of the city. The design is entirely typical of the 1930s, with a modern, yet very dignified frontage which fits in with the surrounding buildings today as well as it has ever done.

Above: A mixture of styles which were not to everyone's taste, this strange amalgam of buildings was joined together by the large Co-operative sign above them. More out of hope than any real conviction, and the outcome mattered little after the construction of the stylish and highly acclaimed *Co-op* property just a short walk away, with its twin towers and simple, but dignified lines. Throughout the region (and, come to that, throughout a large part of the country) the *Co-operative* movement has been responsible for the construction of some excellent properties, many of which found new uses when the *Co-op* grew out of them. This picture was taken to record the decorations put up for the Queens' coronation 1953.

Top: Grey Street in 1953 had a soot-stained appearance typical of most towns and cities in the days before smoke control became a legal requirement in Britain. This picture is one of several taken featuring the city-centre coronation decorations in 1953. The property on the left of the photograph dates from the mid 1800s and was destined to become a branch of Lloyds Bank in more recent times. Further down Grey Street the unmistakable outline of the Theatre Royal is in view. Grey Street was constructed in the 1830s to connect the existing Blackett Street and Dean Street. Most of the splendid buildings on and around Grey Street were constructed in the 1830s and it here that some of the best examples of the work of *Dobson, Grainger, Walker* and *Wardle* can be seen.

NC & J

Above: A casual observer may have been forgiven for perceiving an element of friendly rivalry between the 'Chronicle Office and the adjacent Norwich Union property - were they trying to outdo each other with these elaborate displays? This was the scene along Westgate Road in May 1953. Car buffs may be interested to see the sleek pair of Jowett Javelin saloons outside these offices. Perhaps they were used by representatives of one of the organisations... the Ford Cortina of their day? In modern times they are highly prized collectors items because of their appealing styling and advanced (for the 1950s) 'flat four' engines noted for their reliability, economy and impressive pulling power.

Top right: Even Grey's Monument got the *royal* treatment in June 1953 as decorations for the impending coronation spread throughout the city. Flags, crests, floral displays and mile after mile of ·

bunting gave Newcastle the kind of display that would surely have made neighbouring towns envious. The overhead power cables for the city's trolleybus network give this splendid picture an almost three-dimensional effect. Memories may be stirred by the presence of the old Post Office and *Timothy Whites and Taylors* chemists (later to merge with *Boots*) in the background of the picture.

Right: Winston Churchill visited Newcastle in October 1951 as part of the Conservative Party's campaign in the General Election of that year. This scene shows crowds of supporters lining the route along Grainger Street as a gleaming Rolls Royce carrying Britain's most effective wartime leader sped from the Central Station on its way to Blagdon Hall. Ten days after this picture was taken the conservatives won by a very narrow margin, and Winston Churchill became Prime Minister again - at the age of 76.

NC & J

NC & J

Below: As part of the royal visit to the north east in October 1954 the Queen and the Duke of Edinburgh called at Tynemouth. Special posters were produced by the *Evening Chronicle* and her sister paper *The Journal* to greet the royal couple. Here a group of Tynemouth ladies, well wrapped-up against the autumn weather, make sure that they will be noticed by standing on a suitably positioned wall on the route to be taken by the royal motors.

Bottom: The opening of John Dobson Street was a memorable occasion, marked by a military band marching past the mayor and several local dignitaries on a specially constructed dais. The event took place in the early 1970s and the new thoroughfare did much to ease the congestion along streets like Northumberland Street.

Right: The visit of her Majesty Queen Elizabeth II and H.R.H. the Duke of Edinburgh was a reason for widespread celebration in October 1954. In this picture we see the royal party being greeted by the Mayor and civic dignitaries in Gateshead after they had attended engagements in Newcastle. The royal motorcade had halted on the Tyne Bridge to allow the official welcoming ceremony to take place as near to the boundary with her neighbour as possible. The row of gleaming black Daimlers, Humbers and Rolls Royces made an impressive sight, lined up alongside the guard of honour which was provided by soldiers from the Durham Light Infantry.

NC & J

Power for the people - the Northern Electric story

The world has come full circle for Northern Electric after over 100 years of service to the people of Newcastle and the North East by the Company and its predecessors.

NESCo, the original private sector company, was a pioneer, nationally and internationally, in power generation and supply. The electricity industry was nationalised in 1948 and in this region the North Eastern Electricity Board (NEEB) replaced NESCo and a variety of smaller private and municipal supply organisations. In 1989 NEEB became Northern Electric and in the following year was floated on the stock exchange as a public company as part of the privatisation of the industry.

Then in late 1996 Northern Electric became part of the world-wide energy group CalEnergy, based in the USA and began a new era with Newcastle at the heart of CalEnergy's global operations.

The North East of England has always been at the forefront of developments in electricity - Joseph Swan invented the incandescent electric light bulb and first demonstrated it in 1878 to the Newcastle Chemical Society. At Cragside Hall, in Northumberland, Lord Armstrong, the great Newcastle inventor, shipbuilder and armaments

manufacturer, installed electric lights in 1880, powering them from the world's first domestic hydro-generator. Charles Parsons invented the steam turbine, applied to generate public electricity in Newcastle - another world first. The early electricity companies in the region pioneered a unique integrated regional power network, a model for what was to come elsewhere in the UK and the world.

The Newcastle upon Tyne Electric Supply Company (NESCo) was incorporated in Newcastle in 1889,

Above: Joseph Swan's incandescent lamp.
Below: The Control Room at Dunston 'A' Power Station, with W. Farrel on duty in 1931.

with a capital of £12,000, and by 1890 was supplying electricity from Pandon Dene power station on the east side of the city.

Newcastle had not one but two supply companies, with the Newcastle upon Tyne and District Electric Lighting Company (DISCo) also being formed in 1889. DISCo was Charles Parsons' company, with his steam turbine generators installed at Forth Banks by the river.

The generating station at Pandon Dene initially consisted of two small 75 kilowatt generators. Further generators were later installed, the largest of which was 500 kilowatt . At the power station, coal was delivered by horse and cart. The coal price was three shillings and sixpence per ton.

Charles Merz and others at NESCo saw that there was little future in small-scale localised operations. They also saw the potential for capturing the growing shipbuilding and engineering load of Tyneside for electricity, and so its use for general power purposes began to be actively pursued.

Top: A travelling kitchen of the 1920's.
Right: Pandon Generating Station.

Merz, although working for NESCo, was also consulting engineer to the Walker and Wallsend Company. In 1899 he had begun to plan a power station at Neptune Bank, Wallsend, in association with William McLellan and R P Sloan. Neptune Bank was acquired by NESCo in 1901 and in June of that year began supplying to consumers of the two undertakings.

Its unique position is that it was the first example of a statutory authority in the UK supplying three phase electricity, operating at a pressure of 5,500 volts. Westinghouse had established three phase AC distribution in the USA and this was the form of

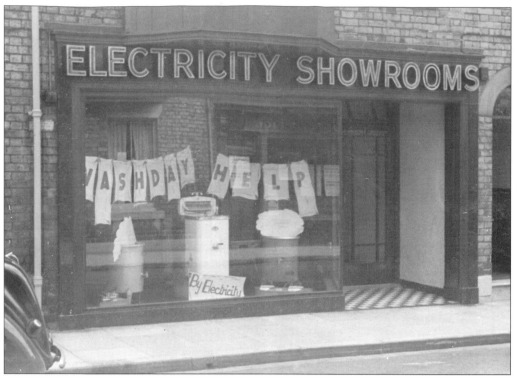

NESCo lauded as the first statutory undertaking in the United Kingdom to supply electricity power in bulk for motive power purposes in works. Neptune Bank originally contained four 700 kilowatt alternators. These were later augmented by two 1500 kilowatt alternators driven by steam turbines manufactured by Parsons, the largest of their type in the world at that time and operating so successfully that the Cunard Company was persuaded to go for propulsion machinery of that type in the famous ship The Mauritania.

power best suited to the new industrial applications of electricity - allowing higher voltages for industrial motors whilst domestic customers received power at lower voltages.

Neptune Bank was much celebrated in its day. It was regarded not only as the inauguration of electric power supply on Tyneside but "the beginning of the era of electric power utilisation all over the kingdom" as The Electrician publication put it, with

Neptune Bank not only led to the rapid expansion of NESCo but it also gave industry on Tyneside an enormous advantage over industry elsewhere. After

Top Left: An electricity showroom in 1935.
Below: Members of Jointers' team waiting for their cue.
Left to right: R. Short (Jointer), T. Redhead (Jointer's Mate), R. Stage (Jointer's Mate).

Left: A very ornate 2000 volt/220 volt kiosk type sub-station. Below: A map of the area in which the Company was authorised to supply electricity.

In 1906, NESCo became the first undertaking to adopt balanced electrical protection gear, of the Merz-Price system, which was significant in improving the reliability and continuity of supply. The principle originally adopted formed the basis of almost every other form of modern automatic electrical protection.

In the same year of 1906 NESCo also became the first to use "metal-clad" switchgear in its substations, thus bringing to Tyneside the important industry of switchgear manufacture to which Reyrolle and Company became so central. In July of that year NESCo installed the first such switchgear at the yard of shipbuilders Swan Hunter.

Neptune Bank NESCo, led the world in power station development for the next thirty years.

Next came a new station on a nearby riverside site at Carville, opened in 1904, which not only supplied the collieries but also the North Eastern Railway for the electrification of their tracks between Newcastle and Tynemouth.

It also supplied power via the High Level Bridge to Gateshead and also to the electrical undertakings then operating in the north east of County Durham via a cable tunnel from Carville to Hebburn, constructed at a depth of 120 feet, length of 1,000 feet and six feet in diameter.

Carville was a landmark in power station design, and secured the reputation of the Newcastle-based consultants and designers Merz and McLellan. It was the largest public supply station in Europe and the first station of any size to be completely powered by Parsons steam turbines, ten times the average size being installed in British stations.

NESCo extended its operations by building a transmission system of both underground cables and overhead lines operating initially at 6 kilowatt. In 1906 the Company became the first undertaking in the country to begin transmission at 20 kilowatt so as to minimise losses over long distances.

Although the North East was perhaps unique in the scale and integration of its supply arrangements, DISCo remained in existence as a separate lighting enterprise and there were several large

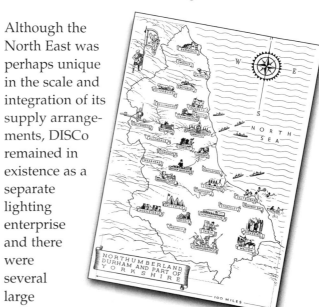

time. This had made it possible to concentrate upon large central generating stations, requiring small reserve plant margins.

By 1905 the average price of electricity sold by NESCo was a fraction over a penny per unit, compared with over four pence just six years earlier. In the first decade of the century sales increased by a factor of 30, far in excess of growth achieved elsewhere. Load factor averaged 45 per cent compared with not much more than 20 per cent in other industrial areas of the country.

The great industrial strength of the North East in the early part of the century was in no small measure due to the widespread availability of reliable power at rates among the cheapest in the world. The efficient and cheap power supply system attracted new industries to the area. A report in the Times in 1905 had compared developments in the North East with those in North America where new industrial loads of significant scale grew up around the cheap hydro-electric power of Niagara.

Nearly half the power at that time was used by collieries and iron mines, a quarter in shipyards, engineering and other works and less than a thirtieth for lighting and domestic uses. The increase in demand during the First World War again made it necessary to extend the generating plant. Carville B was constructed in which the steam pressure was the highest then used by any supply authority in the country.

local authorities in the region who operated their own municipal lighting stations and also provided power for industry locally.

In Newcastle, the corporation developed its own station at Manors to supply its tramways. Nonetheless, some corporations, such as Middlesbrough and Tynemouth, did take supply from companies in the NESCo group for onward distribution using their networks.

From its beginnings in 1889 as a lighting undertaking with an area of only 11 square miles, by the outbreak of the First World War NESCo's system covered 1400 square miles. By then the conversion to three-phase 40 Hz AC was well under way and was the key to large-scale interconnected operation, the largest integrated power system in Europe at the

Another first was the principle of centralised system control, displaying, controlling and operating the high voltage electricity network from a central, co-ordinated control room. The first system control

Above: A linesman precariously perched high above Newcastle. Right: Electrical appliances of their day.

NESCo saw itself as an important leader in both industrial and social progress on Tyneside, and it expressed its confidence in itself and its future through its show piece for excellence, Carliol House, built between 1924 and 1927 and still the headquarters of Northern Electric today. Carliol House was Newcastle's first important modern office building in the modernised classical style of the inter-war period. It incorporated many technical innovations that made it architecturally important, being of reinforced steel construction, a method imported from the USA by the building's architect L J Couves of Newcastle. It incorporated innovative heating and cleaning systems. Sixty tons of electrically heated water were circulated through coiled pipes in the ceilings to heat it and it was the first building to incorporate an integral vacuum cleaning system where the cleaners plugged straight into the wall.

room was in Carville and it attracted the interest of visitors from all over the world. The control diagram took up 960 square feet, and displayed the generating stations, substations and transmission and distribution network. It operated with the help of the Company's own private telephone system.

After the War demand rose steeply and in 1924 NESCo was the first electricity authority in the country to adopt as high a pressure as 66,000 volts for transmission purposes. Lines at this voltage were run between the Tees and Tyne and from the Tyne further north to Bedlington in the heart of the Northumberland coalfield. Where overhead construction was not possible in built-up areas, the Company became the first to make commercial use of underground cable operating at 66 kilowatt.

When the Government set the scene for establishing a national electricity Grid it was NESCo that became the model for co-ordinating and interconnecting power distribution over a wide area.

During the depression of the 1920s there was still considerable growth in electrical demand, including the arrival of electric street lighting on a large scale in cities such as Newcastle and the advent of illuminated shop signs and theatre and cinema lighting.

Top: The control room in the 1950s.
Right: Carliol House, company head office in Market Street.

The high-speed electric lifts were considered to be the most up-to-date in the country, travelling at 430 feet per minute - the fastest, at the time, in Britain and, according to The Newcastle Journal, probably in the world.

There was a luxurious cinema and lecture theatre with seating for 70 which played an important part in educating consumers by means of lectures and demonstrations.

The uniqueness of the building was further underlined by the fact it was faced with Portland Stone rather than Newcastle's traditional sandstone. The grandeur of the exterior was continued inside with the wide use of marble and mahogany. The mixture of Art Deco and stripped classicism with the added distinct Egyptian flavour was popular for commercial buildings of this period.

In recent years a refurbishment programme has restored the reception area to its original elegance and brought the office floors up to 1990s standards.

From the turn of the century the use of electricity in the home, to make life easier and more enjoyable, began to gather pace - first irons, heaters and fans then electric cooking, washing and refrigeration.

The growth of domestic use of electrical appliances and the increased electrical load it bought became an important feature of NESCo's activities, promoted through stylish shops and mobile showrooms. Through the 1930s and beyond the number of connected customers and the amount of electricity they used grew dramatically.

It was also the 1930s which saw the beginning of the growth of electricity in the countryside, boosted by the 1934 Royal Agricultural Society's Show in Newcastle. Lower electricity distribution costs began the great drive towards rural electrification, which resumed after the war and was completed in the 1950s and 1960s.

The great expansion of the network after the war increased the number of staff working for the newly-created NEEB, reaching a peak in 1965 of over 9,000. It was to fall to under 5,000 by the late 1980s and to around 3,500 nowadays, a reflection of increased efficiency and the use of modern technologies.

Immediately post-war, the coal industry was still the most important customer of Northern Electric, taking as much electricity as all the domestic and commercial customers put together. Today the load is much more evenly spread between domestic, commercial and industrial customers, and the new Northern Electric is also a major player in the gas supply market.

The post-war drive to expand the electrical network was extremely successful. By 1952 80% of rural premises were on supply, but the balance of farms and other rural communities was to take longer to connect.

At the same time NEEB was concerned to standardise distribution voltages, which varied throughout its area, and to standardise tariffs so that all domestic customers paid similar rates.

Throughout the 1950s and 1960s prices to customers were below the rate of inflation, despite the costs of developing the network, and there was a significant growth in off-peak electricity, being cheaper for night use.

However all this changed from the early 1970s when the twin shocks of the aftermath of the miners' strikes and the Middle East oil crisis made electricity much more expensive to produce and therefore to distribute to customers, and prices rose accordingly. Suddenly energy conservation was on the agenda and the days of 10% annual growth in sales were at an end.

In the past few years prices have been falling again, quite dramatically and customers of the Northern Electric of today have seen smaller bills, improved service, rising investment and a company that plays a strong and positive role in its local community.

Over one hundred years on, and Northern Electric remains a vitally important company to its region, just as its predecessors were.

Facing page top: The board visit to the meter station in 1985. Bottom left: Enquiry unit staff with visual display terminals in 1975. This page: Rebuilding the line across the Tyne, 1984.

At leisure

Above: On a hot summer's day, what could be better than an afternoon on the beach at Tynemouth? Even better, splashing about in the pool with mam or dad keeping a watchful eye from the chairs and benches around the enclosed bathing area was a pleasurable way to pass a few hours in the long school holidays. People would often walk miles from home to the pool, many taking a picnic to make a real day out of it. This scene dates from August 1958.

Top: The *Travel Bureau* was situated within the Newgate Street Co-op building. It may not look as swish as the modern equivalents located in most department stores (and on virtually every street corner in Newcastle, come to that) but by the time this picture was taken in 1956, interest in the idea of foreign travel was beginning to grow. Of course, holidays in Britain were still the most popular destination and most could be booked from the office along with the railway ticket for the journey. Some of the destinations promoted by the posters here include Denmark, Ulster, France and the Isle of Man.

Left: How many memories began with a journey to Newcastle's Exhibition Park over the years? Here we see the bandstand in the park as it appeared in September 1949 and we are told that the accomplished band of the Coldstream Guards was entertaining an appreciative audience in the last few weeks of the warm weather. The bandstand is of significant historical interest as it was originally built for the 1887 Royal Jubilee Exhibition. In post-war Britain there was precious little spare cash in the pockets of ordinary people to spend on *fripperies.* Opportunities for entertainment and relaxation would be taken where they could, and facilities such as Exhibition Park were highly valued by the residents of the city.

Above: The thrill of the 'aerial chairs' was a big draw, especially to young people, and this picture proves it. We suspect that there has been a bit of dark-room jiggery-pokery, because the faces of the participants as well as the onlookers are in focus. This picture dates from 1947. The Hoppings would have been a welcome pick-me-up for the people of Tyneside at this time, being just two years after the end of the war. Britain was struggling to get back on her economic feet after the immense drain on her resources during the conflict. The government announced severe economic cuts in August 1947 and there was a general air of gloom as the size of the task of regeneration began to sink in. Morale was boosted in November when Princess Elizabeth married Philip Mountbatten.

Top: Intense concentration can be seen on the faces of these visitors to the 1951 Town Moor Festival. It was understandable of course, for there were teddy bears and crockery to be won by those with exceptional ball control. It is interesting to see that the people enjoying the challenge are all adults each determined not to leave the fair empty-handed, and not a child in sight!

All the fun of the fair was the order of the day at the "Hoppings" when this picture was taken. Amazingly, the photograph is around half a century old - for it was taken in 1949. The photograph was carried in the Evening Chronicle in June of that year when it was estimated that over a million visitors attended the Town Moor festival to spend their Race Week leisure time and hard-earned cash over several days of scorching sunshine.

Above: Ready for the off. Row upon row of colourful stalls, each shuttered up against the elements and premature visitors, await the crowds on the Town Moor and the 1957 *Hoppings* festival. Note the building on the right of the photograph with the distinctive domed-roof. It is the *Palace of Arts* in Exhibition Park and dates from 1929. For many years displays of *local* art were shown here to the appreciation of most local art enthusiasts. In later life the building was put to worthwhile use as military transport museum.

Top: A crowded view from the 1955 *Hoppings* on Town Moor. There was nothing very politically correct about 1955 - and this is certainly true of some of the attractions pictured here. Among them is the curiously named *Reluctant Lady* and *Titania,* the 'mountain of flesh and beauty.' If you had a mind to you could pay sixpence and find out 'why men leave home' or, if that was too exciting, you go next door to see the world's smallest woman, *Anita* the living doll.

Left: Looking a bit too similar to Rising Damp's *Rigsby* for comfort, the man on the left of this picture is working hard to drum up customers for his exotic show. The princely sum of sixpence would have taken visitors to the Hoppings on a mystical journey into the unknown in the *Oriental Variety Show.* 'See the amazing Chinese Striptease Girls' proclaimed the banner on the side of the stand. Most visitors to the Town Moor decided against the idea, despite the persuasive patter. The picture dates from 1960.

Well over a hundred people gather round a Northern Tory van on the Town Moor. It was a good year for raincoats in 1963 - virtually everyone here seems to wearing one! The gent speaking from the specially modified van, with its nifty open hatch must have had a good line in banter to compete with the colourful attractions on the rest of the moor. Everyone is agog - with the exception of the young lad in the foreground who is more interested in the work of our photographer.

NC & J

Wartime

NC & J

Above: A direct hit on this terrace of houses caused three of them to be reduced to a pile of rubble. This raid took place in April 1941, just before the launch of *War Savings Week.* At around this time there was intense activity as virtually every empty workshop in the area (and throughout Britain) was converted into mini-munitions factories. Women became increasingly involved in wartime production and the maintenance of services on the home front. Britain, unlike her enemy, was operating under a siege economy.

Houses reduced to rubble after the December 1941 raid on the Matthew Bank area of Newcastle. It is impossible for people today to understand the feelings of the survivors of such an air-raid, surveying the rubble as dawn broke on the following day. Attempts were made to salvage as many possessions as possible from the remains of the houses, though extreme care had to be taken not to be injured by falling masonry from the wrecked buildings.

Above: These houses in the Keyes Gardens area of Matthew Bank were once the pride and joy of the residents there. Several houses were completely destroyed in the bombing raid of December 1941, but a much greater number suffered more superficial damage in the form of broken glass and damaged roof tops over a very wide area. In true northern style the raid brought out the best in the friends and neighbours of those affected, and everyone rallied round the victims with numerous offers of support and any assistance they could give.

Top: Utter devastation was the result of a night-time bombing raid on the Matthew Bank Estate in December 1941. The raid caused widespread damage here and in South Gosforth and caused the loss of five lives. The raid coincided with the Japanese attack on Pearl Harbour which brought the United States into the conflict. Earlier in 1941 Hitler had attacked Russia and found himself fighting on two fronts. At the time this picture was taken the effect of the war *on the home front* was beginning to increase. White bread was becoming scarce and there was widespread talk of coal rationing. Millions of women began to be involved in all types of production and the public utilities and many parks and open-spaces were turned over to vegetable production.

Above: Spring 1943, and workmen and residents attempt to salvage what they can after an enemy bombing raid on The Oval in the St. Anthony's area of the city. Newcastle did not experience the widespread devastation seen in Manchester, Liverpool or the Midlands, but when the raids did occur they inevitably caused serious disruption for the people concerned. London sustained the loss of around 30,000 lives during the conflict - around half the total number of bombing casualties for the whole of Britain. *Anderson* shelters had been distributed in the first year of the war and no doubt saved many lives as a consequence. After only a few months it was thought that around half the families issued with the shelters stopped using them as they became totally waterlogged. *Morrison* shelters later became available and consisted of a wire 'cage' which was positioned in a safe place inside the household and in which people would sleep (if possible!) during night time raids.

Right: The smiling faces and happy expressions say it all, for this was one of the hundreds of street parties and celebratory events held throughout Tyneside to celebrate the end of the war. These residents of Lambert Square in Coxlodge had pulled out all the stops to provide a spread that would be remembered for as long as they lived. Some of the children in the picture were so young that their only memories would have been of wartime, and it is sobering to think that most of them will be at least 60 years of age at the time of writing, and many of the adults will no longer be with us. This photograph was taken on May 8th 1945.

NC & J

Around the city centre

Right: The whole of the city centre was decorated with flags and bunting in May 1935 for the Silver Jubilee of King George V. The photograph dates from May 1935 and shows the decorations along Newcastle's main shopping area, Northumberland Street. George V had succeeded Edward VII in 1910 and went on to reign for just one more year until his death in 1936. Edward VIII reigned for a short time afterwards but opted for the love of American divorcee Mrs Wallace Simpson in preference to the responsibilities of State, when faced with an ultimatum from the government of the day. Edward sloped off to France and assumed the title *Duke of Windsor* in December 1936. His brother became George VI and, with his queen Elizabeth, went on to achieve tremendous popularity in the turbulent years that followed.

Inset: This very rare photograph from 1938 features a street in the centre of the city on a July afternoon. This is Northumberland Road and the photographer was looking in an easterly direction when he took the picture. The heavily shaded windows on the left belong to the *Marcus* fur retailing business. They have long since vacated the property which went on to be occupied by the Abbey National Building Society.

On the right of the picture an open-topped chara can be seen. Many of these popular vehicles, including this one, had a canvass roof which could be drawn back to give the passengers an open-air ride to their destination. Ideal for day trippers on their way to the coast, eager to exploit the rare opportunity of some fresh air in their lungs!

Below: A slightly elevated view taken in Grainger Street. It dates from late 1952 and shows a variety of delightful motor vehicles making their way up and down this busy street. In the centre of the picture a *Bainbridges* Bedford 'luton' bodied truck approaches the position of the camera. These vehicles were very popular at the time. Drivers on long journeys requiring an overnight stop would often tell their friends that they were staying at the 'Luton Hotel' - a reference to the small compartment over the cab of the lorry from which the term 'luton van' was derived. Here they would sleep as best they could in a sleeping bag before resuming their journey.

NC & J

ROYAL GREETINGS
FROM NORTHUMBERLAND STREET

A photograph dating from May 1953 and showing that the decorations for the coronation of the new Queen were already beginning to brighten up the centre of Newcastle. The location is Market Street and it can be seen that the major stores, including Binns were taking the event very seriously.

Above: Many changes have taken place in this area since this roof top view of Northumberland Road was recorded. The photograph was taken in May 1956. College Street can be seen on the left of the picture. The distinctive black and white arches in the centre of the picture indicate the location of Rossleigh's Garage. They sold several different marques including Triumph and Jaguar. A multi-storey car park now stands on the site they occupied. Beyond Rossleigh's Garage the Olympia Cinema can be seen. The Olympia opened in 1909 and had a seating capacity of 1500. More mature readers may recall the deafening sound created by heavy rainstorms on the tin roof of the cinema. The establishment closed in 1961 after a final showing of the Peter Sellers film *The Millionairess.* For around a decade later the property was used as a warehouse by British Home Stores until it was pulled down in 1971.

Top: The busy route into Newcastle via the High Level Bridge and along St. Nicholas Street attracted commercial developers in the middle of the nineteenth century. The most obvious example of their work is shown here, the impressive facade of St. Nicholas Buildings as designed by William Parnell. This picture was taken in September 1952 and shows the dark walls of St. Nicholas Buildings over forty years before the idea of redeveloping the site had been put forward. The hard, tightly packed cobble stones - so slippery in the wet, and the selection of curvaceous saloon cars from the late 1940s and early 1950s adds atmosphere to the nostalgic scene.

The corner of Northumberland Street and Brunswick Place was the location chosen for this photograph. Northumberland Street was lavishly decorated for the celebrations which were held for the coronation in May and June 1953. The large store on the left is Fenwicks of course, and it is obvious that they had made a special effort to demonstrate their support for the new monarch, with an enormous portrait of Her Majesty with the words 'Long may she reign' beneath it. The impressive facade was added to the original building in 1913.

Above: *A scene of virtual chaos at the junction of Blackett Street and Northumberland Street, with almost every form of motorised transport represented in this splendid photograph. The large, distinctive Burton's building can be seen on the left. This was a huge monument to the success of the tailoring organisation which had similar (though generally smaller) stores on almost every high street in the country. Trolley buses are featured here along with a No.26 diesel double-decker en-route to Pelaw in the foreground. The photograph was taken in June 1953, a time when the whole of Britain was celebrating the coronation of Queen Elizabeth II in Westminster Abbey.*

NC & J

Above: Still easily recognisable as the Collingwood Street, Westgate Road and Neville Street area of the city to modern residents despite there having been some very major construction work here since this picture was taken in 1959. The buildings on the left of the picture, including the old offices of the *Newcastle Chronicle and Journal* and *Norwich Union* have been pulled down to make way for a huge office block. Most of the buildings which remain have, at some time, had the bulk of the black soot removed from their exterior, giving the streets along here a much brighter appearance. The five storey building housing Barclays Bank was notable for the magnificent plasterwork on the ground floor banking hall. The building was opened in 1905.

Top: Construction work prompted the taking of this photograph in April 1971. This major office development was nearing completion along Pilgrim Street.

Left: One of the busiest streets in the city is featured in this elevated view from 1959. Northumberland Street, with the junction of Blackett Street and Pilgrim Street. Some policeman have gone to the aid of the long lines of traffic as pedestrians do their best to squeeze in between the cars and buses in this nostalgic lunchtime scene. Northumberland Street has been the town's most important shopping street since the 1920s. For many decades, among them the time featured here, it was on the main through-route from London to Edinburgh. The fine old Burton's building has made way in more recent times for the Monument Mall shopping centre, strengthening the position of Northumberland Street's position as one of Britain's busiest shopping streets outside London.

Newgate Street had a familiar, but significantly different appearance in 1961 when this picture was taken. The exterior of the Newcastle Co-op building looked in need of a thorough cleaning, and no wonder after years of exposure to the belching exhausts from the heavy traffic beside it. On the left of the picture, at No. 118 Newgate Street, the Chancellor's Head public house can be seen. It was demolished along with other buildings in the area in 1971 to make way for the new Eldon Square shopping development.

Above: This very nostalgic image from 1960 features the Haymarket with the new towering King's College Physics block dominating the skyline. The picture affords an excellent view of the Haymarket ABC cinema which was built in 1933. With less than 1300 seats it was a medium sized establishment managed independently and noted for the special *Western Electric* sound system and the quality of the upstairs cafe which was run by *Hunter's the Bakers*. Within a few years of the opening of the cinema it was extensively modified and the capacity increased to around 2000. The South African war memorial 'The Winged Victory' looks out across the scene from the centre of the picture.

Top: Part of the city wall in the Bath Lane area of Newcastle, with the neatly laid out paved area, raised flower beds and wooden benches had been recently renovated when this scene was captured in March 1961. Referred to as 'an oasis within the city' by the planners it was intended as an area of rest and relaxation for tired shoppers and passers-by. The Essoldo cinema can just be seen at the top of the photograph. It had opened in 1938, the first feature being *The Hurricane* starring Dorothy Lamour. The Essoldo had the distinction of being the first cinema in Newcastle to show the block-busting movie *Gone with the Wind*. The cinema changed name many times, particularly in the last few years of its operation. It finally closed in January 1990, the last film shown there being *Shirley Valentine*. The building was pulled down in 1991.

Above: Work was well under way on the new route through the centre of the city - John Dobson Street, when this picture was taken in 1969. The section linked St. Mary's Place and Northumberland Road and was designed to ease traffic congestion, particularly on the north-south route through the centre of Newcastle. When opened, south-bound traffic could turn left into St. Mary's Place, go down the link road to Northumberland Road and back along it into Northumberland Street. As a consequence it was possible to make most of the traffic on the busy Northumberland Street mainly south-bound buses and delivery vehicles. John Dobson Street cost £1,200,000 and provided a link between the central motorway system and the city centre. The pedestrian deck at the south end of the works was over 300ft long and up to 90ft wide.

Left: This fascinating view of the Bigg Market and the buildings beyond dates from 1964. It was taken by an intrepid photographer from the roof of the old Town Hall. Market trading was in full swing on the street below, and several familiar retail names can be seen along the edges of this busy and historic thoroughfare. H. Samuels the jewellers can be seen in the distance with James Allan and Freemans nearer to the position the of the camera. The old Co-operative building can be seen further along, looking rather clumsy in comparison with its modern equivalent. Beyond the Co-op sign is the imposing structure which is the towering Newgate House. The *old* Town Hall, from where this photograph was taken, was an imposing building constructed in a five year period beginning in 1868. It was replaced in the 1970s by a modern office block.

People in the news

Right: The Mayor of Gateshead, Councillor B.N. Young greeted the royal party when they visited the area in October 1954. Also pictured is Lord Lawson, Lord Lieutenant of County Durham, speaking with the Duke of Edinburgh. The Queen seems relaxed and youthful as she looks towards the civic officials waiting to welcome her to Gateshead less than 18 months after her coronation. On the right of the picture, in the distance, a newsreel cameraman can be seen recording the event for cinema audiences everywhere. The High Level Bridge, which was constructed between 1846 and 1849 provides an appropriate backdrop for this picture for it was officially opened some 95 years earlier by Queen Victoria.

Inset: We would normally expect Queen Elizabeth the Queen Mother to be more at home on the racecourse than on the bowling green. But this delightful photograph from 1936 when she was the Duchess of York shows her in relaxed and happy mood as she confidently launches a wood across a Tyneside bowling green. Her Majesty was just 36 years of age when the picture was taken, over sixty years ago. She was accompanying her husband, The Duke of York, later King George VI, on a tour of the North East.

Below: An historic picture from around half a century ago. The exact date was November 5th 1949 and the location was the Burnden Park home of Bolton Wanderers, where Newcastle United were visiting for their clash with the Lancashire club. It was smiles all round when one of the outstanding characters of the Second World War visited the venue and met players and officials from both sides. The hero in question was Field Marshal Viscount Montgomery. He is pictured meeting the players before the match, among them being Newcastle's local hero, *Jackie Milburn.*

NC & J

NC & J

Above: Long before his name had been associated with *This is Your Life,* Eamon Andrews achieved popularity as a radio journalist and boxing commentator. He became a national celebrity thanks to the dawn of the *Television Age,* and, like his modern equivalents today, earned some valuable spending money *on the side* from his activities opening shops and attending functions whenever this was possible. In this picture Eamon is about to cut a television-shaped cake to mark the opening of this new T.V. and radio store on Shields Road. It was taken in July 1956. Without doubt he was the *Terry Wogan* of his day with his charismatic Irish accent, square jaw and film star looks.

Top: *My name's Michael Caine.* And not a lot of people knew that the film being made on Tyneside would go on to be regarded as the definitive British cult movie. It was released in 1971. This publicity photograph was taken in the shadow of the giant tanker the Esso Hibernia at Wallsend. The plot revolved around a racketeer who travelled to Tyneside to avenge his brother's death. For the time it had sex and violence in exceptionally liberal amounts with brutality to match. The film was based on a novel, *Jack's Return Home* by Ted Lewis and starred Michael Caine, John Osborne, Ian Hendry and Brit Eckland. Coronation Street lovers will remember Brian Mosley's excellent performance in the film. He went on to play *Alf Roberts,* the hen-pecked grocer in the best soap opera *in the world.*

NC & J

Above: More mature readers will be familiar with the characters in this symbolic photograph. The background shows a combination of 'old' and 'new' Newcastle, stretching from the roof of Welbar House in Gallowgate, where the picture was taken, to the distant horizon. In the centre of the photograph is T. Dan Smith, with William Rodgers the (then) Under Secretary of State, Department of Economic Affairs (left) and J.G. Robinson, the chairman of the Region's Economic Planning Board. This mid-1960s photograph was taken long before the *Poulson* scandal which rocked the world of local politics. T. Dan Smith was arrested on October 5th 1972 on serious corruption charges for which he was later convicted and imprisoned.

This dramatic photograph shows preparatory work well underway prior to the construction of the new St. James's Station - all part of the creation of the Tyneside Metro. This considerable chunk of Gallowgate had been pulled down by Blair Demolition, the Darlington-based company brought in to complete the task. During the work part of the outer wall of St. James's Park football club had to be partly demolished and the turnstiles taken away while deep piles were driven into the ground during the close season.

The Changing city

Bottom: In the days before virtually every street corner seemed to have a multi-storey car park built upon it, it was common practice to use demolition sites as temporary car parks. This photograph shows the site which would later become the location of the new Town Hall near St. Thomas Street with workmen fighting a losing battle trying to spread ash on the deep mud to make it possible for motors to park here. The photograph was taken in December 1959, a year which saw the first 'live' journey into space (by a monkey!) in preparation for the space race which would dominate the technological revolution in the following decade.

Below: Newcastle Royal Victoria Infirmary is featured here in a photograph taken in 1950. The rows of teardrop-bodied cars are the main clue to the date of the picture. This trusty servant of the city has existed since 1906. It was opened by King Edward VII and replaced the original Infirmary which had existed on the Forth Banks site since 1753. Donations from the Hall and the Armstrong families totalling over £200,000 had made the construction of the new infirmary possible. At the time this picture was taken the National Health Service had been in existed only a short time. It had been founded by the National Health Act in November 1946.

NC & J

Above: April 1965, and the Pilgrim Street roundabout was open to traffic on the north and east sides, though a tremendous amount of work remained in the centre of the new development. This was to be one of the last images produced showing the houses in the centre of the roundabout which would soon be swept away and replaced by a concrete office block. The picture was taken from the roof of Carliol House; Carliol Square can be seen directly below the position of the photographer. In the distance the distinctive shape of the crown of St. Nicholas Cathedral dominates the skyline.

Left: Who could have guessed that the area around Pilgrim Street would be transformed by the construction of a massive tower block when they looked at the area in the mid-1960s? This giant structure can be seen growing on top of its two sturdy concrete legs in a picture from the summer of 1968. This was the year that saw the introduction of decimal currency in Britain as well as the tragic assassination of Martin Luther King. Another dastardly murder took place just three days after this picture was taken when Senator Robert Kennedy was gunned down by Jordanian Arab Sirhan Bishara Sirhan in California.

Sporting life

Bottom: A sea of happy faces looks towards the camera as the match between Newcastle United and Blackpool gets underway. This was the 1951 F.A. Cup Final at Wembley and the Newcastle fans are characteristically enjoying the occasion. There are lots of interesting details in the picture capable of bringing back a few memories; notice the gents in the centre of the picture on the front row of the terrace. They had come well-equipped for the game with sandwiches in a metal biscuit tin and a few bottles of beer (complete with glasses!) all neatly laid out before them. How times have changed!

Below: Newcastle United football fans enjoyed themselves in London before taking the short trip up to Wembley to watch the 1951 cup final. They are seen here with fans from the opposing team, Blackpool, in Trafalgar Square. The scene looks charmingly good-humoured. It would have been noisy with the cheering and constant racket from the wooden rattles.

The fans turned out in force on the streets of Newcastle when the triumphant team toured the area after winning the F.A. Cup in 1951. Excited fans began to break ranks and run after the curvaceous coaches carrying their heroes along Westgate Road, past the Norwich Union Insurance offices and adjacent home of the Newcastle Chronicle and Journal Ltd. Fans of both sexes and all ages had turned out to pay homage to their favourite team and those lucky enough to work in one of the properties which lined the route dangled precariously out from every window ledge in a bid to get a better view.

Above: 'Welcome Hyem Canny Lads' was the message that echoed the thoughts in the minds of the folk of Tyneside as they awaited the arrival of the cup winners after the 1951 cup success. The 1951 final had been dubbed by the papers 'the Matthews Final' in recognition of the fact that Blackpool's Stanley Matthews had never won the F.A. Cup in his distinguished 20 year career. This was likely to be his last chance. Outside Newcastle it seemed as if the whole nation wanted Blackpool to win so that Matthews could realise his dream. Two goals from Tyneside hero Jackie Milburn would ensure that the cup was brought back to the north east and prevent England's favourite footballer from achieving his ambition. This is a fairly rare 1950s photograph of the interior of the Central Station which has stood on this spot since it was opened by Queen Victoria in 1850.

Inset: This party of Newcastle United supporters had travelled to the capital for the F.A. Cup Final clash with Manchester City. It was May 1955 and the supporters had travelled down on one of the many special trains for the match and were clearly filled with excitement and anticipation of what the afternoon's sport might bring. This photograph was taken near Trafalgar Square and these noisy, but good-humoured fans were happy to express their feelings for the 'Chronicle photographer who had travelled down with them for the occasion. In the mid-1950s the world of professional football was rather different to what it is now. For instance, players wages had a strictly enforced upper limit - in 1954 this was just £15 per week! The season prior to this cup final had been a difficult one for the Newcastle team. The training techniques employed by new manager Duggie Livingstone did not meet with the approval of the more mature members of the squad. In later years Jackie Milburn recalled a training session at which Livingstone went to great lengths to show the great Bobby Mitchell how to kick the ball with his left foot. It was the kind of leadership that did more harm than good, and few insiders were surprised when Livingstone left the club shortly after the Cup Final.

Left: A sense of urgency gripped the crowd of supporters and well-wishers are they struggled to keep up with the open-topped coaches carrying the Newcastle footballers. The F.A. Cup is clearly in view, it had been passed around the players as they took turns to hold it aloft to the delight of the cheering throng. The scene was recorded after the 1-0 win over Arsenal in the 1952 F.A. Cup competition, leading to them becoming known locally as 'the team of the century.' Behind the scenes at Newcastle United people were not as content as they might have been. The backbone of the playing staff consisted mainly of local lads who were motivated by their loyalty to the fans, to each other and to the club itself. They had cost the club little and cared less for the men who occupied the boardroom, but the likes of Len Shackleton, Jackie Milburn, Bobby Mitchell and Jack Fairbrother performed for the love of their fans and for the love of football itself.

NC & J

Above: A packed scene along Grey Street in May 1955. It was a heroes welcome for the Newcastle United team's return from Wembley as thousands of supporters and well-wishers came into the city to applaud and cheer *their* team. The left of the photograph is dominated by the huge dark base of Grey's Monument, supporting the 130ft high tribute to the Charles, Earl Grey. The monument has marked this spot since 1838 and was built to honour the man who had devoted so much energy to the 1832 Reform Act. The premises of Mawson Swan and Morgan Ltd and Lloyds Bank can also be seen in the picture. The year 1955 is also remembered for the terrible Le-Mans race circuit disaster in which 70 spectators lost their lives when a Mercedes racing car crashed into the crowd.

Left: This action-packed picture has been seen many times and will be familiar to those interested in the past glory and achievements of Newcastle United. It captures the moment when the team's most famous player Jackie Milburn scored the first goal of the match in the 1955 Wembley final against Manchester City.

Remarkably the goal was scored in the very first minute of the match by Tyneside's hero, sending the 30,000 Newcastle fans who had travelled to London into a state of ecstacy. Even more remarkably, Newcastle's manager Dugald Livingstone had proposed to drop Milburn from the Wembley team in the days leading up to the match, and it was only the intervention of the directors that put his name back on the team sheet. Back on Tyneside, thousands of lucky fans were able, for the first time, to watch their club compete in the Cup Final on television.

Top left: The distinctive Wembley domes can be seen peeping over the roof of the stand in this 1955 F.A. Cup clash between Manchester City and Newcastle United. Newcastle went on to win the game by three goals to one and receive a rapturous welcome when they returned home to Tyneside. The Wembley success put the club in the record books as the only club to be undefeated at Wembley, to score the quickest goal in a final match, the first club to take part in ten finals, and for the most wins (five) at Wembley.

Bird's eye view

Below: An aerial view of High West Jesmond looking towards High Heaton and Longbenton which dates from 1957. Matthew Bank can be seen on the left, alongside the busy A189 Haddricksmill Road. In the distance, Benton Park Road runs from left to right, past the Longbenton Estate and the Ministry of Pensions buildings which, despite being greatly expanded and renamed D.S.S. is still referred to as the *Ministry* by local people. Also running left to right is the *Coxlodge Wagonway,* a pleasant country walk in modern times as it was when this picture was taken. Much nearer to the camera, and almost below the aircraft, Jesmond Dene House is in view. A similar scene today would be dominated by the Freeman Hospital building and grounds.

> "THE ELDON SQUARE DEVELOPMENT CHANGED THE CITY'S SKYLINE FOREVER"

WP

Above: August 1957, and a 'plane can be heard slowly making it's way across the sky above central Newcastle at an altitude of 2,000 feet. On board a photographer records the scene below and, in this picture, uses St. Thomas' Church and the Haymarket War Memorial as the centrepiece for the composition. The Haymarket bus station is clearly in view as is the busy retail heart of the city long before the Eldon Square development changed the appearance of the *top end* of the city forever.

Left: Town Moor and the *Hoppings* as they have rarely been seen in a picture taken in 1957. Exhibition Park and the Military Transport Museum can be seen in the distance, but it is the straight, tree-lined *Great North Road* adjacent to the busy fairground site which captures the imagination. From a height of 2,000 feet the scene looks far more orderly than it did on the ground, with showmen's stalls and attractions laid out in a neat oval shape and their mobile living accommodation parked in a generally orderly manner behind them. The thousands of visitors who had flocked to the fair look like ants as they move from stall to stall in the summer sunshine.

Below: This aerial view of central Newcastle dates from 1957. In the distance it is just possible to make out the course of the Tyne. In the centre of the picture the Haymarket and St. Thomas' Church (completed 1830) can be seen, with the broad thoroughfares of Percy Street and Northumberland Street leading away from the camera. St. James' Park is just in view on the right of the picture, below Leazes Park. Looking towards St. Mary's Place and Sandyford Road it is possible to see the foundations of the new Civic Centre being laid and surrounding terraces of houses in the process of demolition. The Civic Centre was conceived in the early 1950s after being designed by George Kenyon the City Architect. Building work was completed in 1969 and the overall cost was around £5 million.

WP

Shopping spree

Bottom: A delightful picture from April 1930, showing the busy corner of Clayton Street and Newgate Street. The Burton's store still had a very new appearance at this time and notices in the upstairs windows indicate that the firm was trying to attract business tenants to the space on the upper floors. Woodhouses, the furnishers, can be seen further along the street. Note the vertical sign on the pole on the left indicting the location of this *Tram Stop* - an interesting 'sign of the times' which emphasises the fact that the picture was taken around seventy years ago.

Below: The Grainger Market has always been a favourite place from which to choose the centrepiece of Christmas lunch. This was as true in 1936, as this picture shows, as it was in later years. The ladies in this group had spotted the photographer as he was about to take the picture for the following days' *Evening Chronicle.* The long legs protruding from the wrapping give the impression that one lucky family was going to be having flamingo for their Christmas lunch.

NC & J

Above: This delightfully nostalgic scene dates from August 1952 and shows a busy shopping scene along Market Street. The photograph is dominated the imposing facade of *Bainbridges.* The popular store began life as a single shop at 29 Market Street, owned and created by Mr Emerson Muschamp Bainbridge and specialising in drapery. The business grew and developed over the years and was passed down through future generations of the Bainbridge family. By 1938 this impressive frontage was in place, and departments in the store extended right through to the Bigg Market. By 1976 the store relocated to its present Eldon Square site. Later Binn's took over the building but that store ceased trading from this site in 1995.

NC & J

Left: Grainger Street seldom looked so handsome as it did in this delightful view from 1953. Royal decorations added an air of optimism to the city - long overdue in the difficult times experienced after the end of the war. The coronation was a much-needed excuse for a national celebration, and the people of Tyneside grasped it eagerly. Notice the little lad in the centre of the picture; despite being only about eight years old he is smartly turned out in a short-trousered suit as he walks along Grainger Street with his mam. We would be proud of him today, though *grandad* would probably have clipped his ear for walking with his hands in his pockets! Notice too that these were also the days when it was considered *more respectable* for ladies to wear a hat when out shopping.

Above: This picture was taken from the corner of Newgate Street, looking down Grainger Street, in June 1953. The area had been lavishly decorated for the coronation of Queen Elizabeth II which took place on June 2nd. The scene is bound to bring back memories 1950s Newcastle for anyone who was around at that time. Familiar names abound on the picture, from H. Samuel's the jewellers on the right, to Milletts, Campbell's and the *Fine Art Galleries* of Mawson, Swan and Morgan Ltd. Passers-by seem quite unaware of the photographer, and would have been astounded to think that their image was being recorded for us to see almost half a century later!

NC & J

Above: The unmistakable interior of the Grainger Market at Christmas time. The picture dates from December 1955 and shows proud assistants at Hector Hall's stall. An advert in the *Evening Chronicle* urged shoppers to visit the stall to see their grand display of Christmas poultry from local farms. The Grainger Market opened in October 1835 after an impressive opening ceremony attended by over 2000 people. The market incorporated a Vegetable and Butchery Market which was said to be the largest in Britain. It had fourteen entrances and the 243 shops covered an area of more than two acres.

Top: A rainy day along Grainger Street was the setting for this 1954 photograph. It may just be possible to make out the sign on the left of the picture marking the location of the Grainger Tea Rooms. In the far distance the hazy grey column supporting the statue of Earl Grey is just visible. On the right the Bainbridges Grainger Street entrance is shown next to the prominent Finneys sign. Finneys were seed growers and bulb importers according to the enormous sign on the front of their building. Readers may remember visiting the other shops along Grainger Street - such as Murtons, Walkovers (the shoe shop), John H. Dean, Dunn and Co., and Brown's.

Left: Northumberland Street in 1953 with *British Home Stores* and *Marcos* the fur retailers shown on the right. There was an inevitable dilemma as a result of the street's tremendous retailing activity and the fact that Northumberland Street was the main through route for the busy London to Edinburgh road. Pedestrianisation and the construction of the central motorway would change all that in later years to the benefit of shoppers and travellers alike.

Above: Those with 'eagle eyes' may just be able to make out the advertising sign on the Y.M.C.A. building (built in 1896) in the far distance. The sign promotes the use of *Will's Capstan Cigarettes* and was positioned here more out of co-incidence than any attempt at a shrewd marketing drive on the youth market. The Burton's building is shown in all its glory - it was pulled down in order to make way for the Monument Mall shopping development. The distinctive clock on the left of the photograph belongs to *Northern Goldsmith's*. Perhaps it was the presence of Northern Goldsmith's across the street which prompted the cheeky sign on the fascia of H. Samuel's which read: 'H. Samuel Empire's Largest Jeweller."

Top: Pedestrians take their life in their hands as they cross the busy road at Marlborough Crescent, long before the days when white zig-zags warned of the approach to a crossing. The ladies in the picture may have been *en-route* to the shops and all are well-wrapped up against the cold weather of late October. The picture was taken in 1956.

Try Farnons First was the message on the illuminated sign outside one of Newcastle's favourite stores. John Farnon established his drapers business in 1867. The Nun Street store did brisk business in this central location only a stones' throw from the Grainger Market. This picture was taken in October 1950. The brightly-lit Farnons store cheers up an otherwise gloomy street, curiously devoid of shoppers in the run up to the Christmas rush.

A crowded scene from 1958, when motor traffic was still allowed to make its way up and down Northumberland Street. The photograph is dominated by the large Woodhouses store on the right as we look up this busy retail thoroughfare. Beside it there are other familiar trading names, such as Van Allan, and the Metropole Cafe. Overhead there is evidence of the trolley bus era in the form of the taut power cables which formed a spiders' web of wires carrying electricity to the vehicles below. By the time this picture was taken there were growing health concerns in towns and cities like Newcastle about the fumes created by vehicles such as the ones featured here. This concern, along with the demands of national retailers would lead to the creation of inner ring roads and traffic-free areas designed to make our lives safer and healthier.

Bottom: Once described as the most important shopping street outside the capital, Northumberland Street has succeeded in attracting the most prestigious retail names to it for at least 70 years. This photograph was taken in 1958, a time when the air overhead was filled with electric cables for the trolley bus service, and the air at street level was filled with dangerous fumes from the hundreds of motor vehicles which squeezed through the busy bottleneck in the days before pedestrianisation. The picture is dominated by the tall dark building, Pearl Assurance House at the corner of Northumberland Street and New Bridge Street. It was also known as Cook's Corner by many locals because of the travel agents of that name which stood on the corner. The seven-storey building was designed by William Hope and built between 1902 and 1904. Hope was a nationally renowned theatre designer. Sadly this fine building was pulled down in the 1960s.

Below: The West Road branch of the Newcastle Co-operative Society's store is featured in this photograph from April 1956. On Tyneside, as in the rest of the country, the Co-op had been the dominant force in retailing for as long as anyone could remember. The shopping habits of the British public had changed dramatically over the years, affected by trends in car ownership, and the growth in disposable income and suburban supermarkets. Corner shops have experienced many ups and downs in their popularity over the period covered by this book. During the 1960s and '70s many competed effectively by extending their opening hours and becoming what we now refer to as convenience stores. The Co-op has always had a policy of locating their shops in areas convenient for their customers and this outlet on West Road is a good example of it.

Above: A bird's eye view of bustling Clayton Street, looking from the Westgate Road end towards Newgate Street. The picture dates from January 1959, but Clayton Street itself was laid out in the 1830s. Traffic restrictions were either non-existent or widely ignored if this scene is anything to go by. There were many large stores along Clayton Street, all competing with each other for the attention of shoppers with their large vertical signs. Among these were Hardy's, Shephards, Marshall's, Simmons and Gordons. Two weeks after this picture was taken, on February 3rd 1959, the popular American pop singer, Buddy Holly, was killed in a tragic plane crash.

Right: Westgate Road is featured in a photograph from 1971. The impressive Barclays Bank *(Foreign Branch)* building can be seen on the right, making the best possible use of the narrow triangular site it occupies. Al the motor vehicles in the picture are typical of what one might expect to see on the roads, with the exception of the Ford Prefect saloon nearest to the camera. This vehicle with its wooden floor and rubber-panelled roof was probably manufactured in the late 1940s, when raw materials were still in short supply after the war. Several well-known businesses can be seen along Westgate Road, including the Provincial Building society, R.S. Boulton the tobacconists and Woolf's.

NC & J

Bottom: *Andrews for Canada, Dollars for Britain* was the message that the management at Scott and Turners wanted to get across to the people of Tyneside. They are seen here outside the works, beneath the Union Flag and beside the fleet of trucks which were packed with tons of the effective remedy, set to be exported to Canada. It was July 1952 and the British economy, which had been so slow to recover after the war, needed every export order it was possible to get.

Right: The procession of open-backed trucks makes it way along a busy town centre Street in July 1952. The organisers were proud of their achievement in securing a large export order to Canada - signs on the lorries indicate that it was for '140,000 tins' and that's a lot of *liver salts* by anyone's standards! Further along the street the *Grand Hotel* is visible, near the corner on which Barclays Bank stands.

Below: Here, the convoy can be seen making its way down Northumberland Street when it toured the area to promote its export success. The famous powder was made by Scott and Turners at their *Tin Box Factory.* At the time this picture was taken the health of people nearer home was on the minds of the public. Air pollution was the culprit - there were no controls at this time (though they were soon to follow) and over 4,000 Londoners suffered a premature death after pollutants became trapped in the atmosphere in one of the worst instances of 'smog' on record.

On the move

NC & J

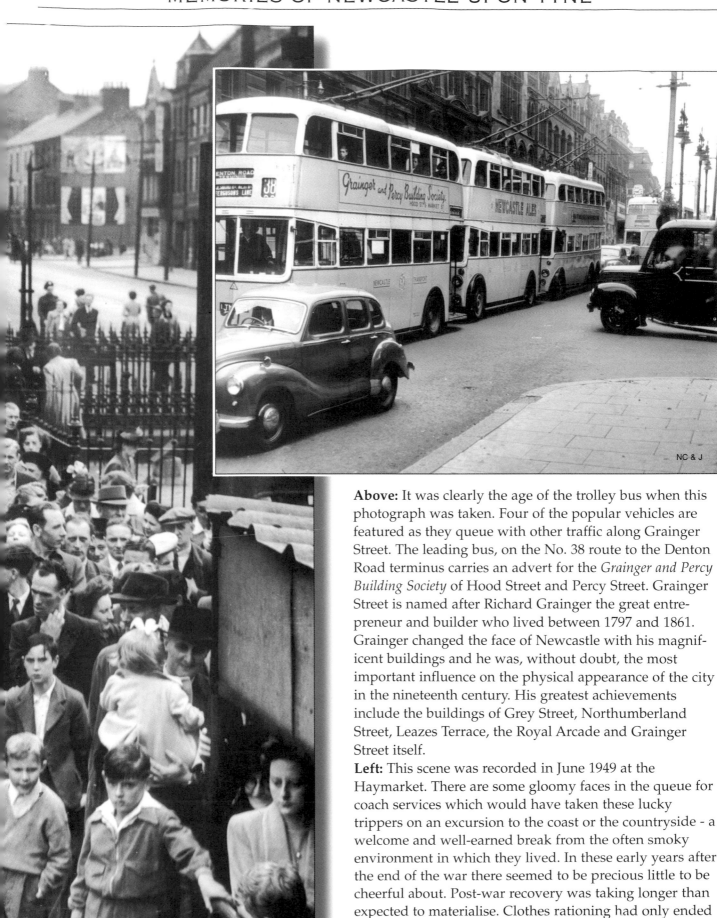

NC & J

Above: It was clearly the age of the trolley bus when this photograph was taken. Four of the popular vehicles are featured as they queue with other traffic along Grainger Street. The leading bus, on the No. 38 route to the Denton Road terminus carries an advert for the *Grainger and Percy Building Society* of Hood Street and Percy Street. Grainger Street is named after Richard Grainger the great entrepreneur and builder who lived between 1797 and 1861. Grainger changed the face of Newcastle with his magnificent buildings and he was, without doubt, the most important influence on the physical appearance of the city in the nineteenth century. His greatest achievements include the buildings of Grey Street, Northumberland Street, Leazes Terrace, the Royal Arcade and Grainger Street itself.

Left: This scene was recorded in June 1949 at the Haymarket. There are some gloomy faces in the queue for coach services which would have taken these lucky trippers on an excursion to the coast or the countryside - a welcome and well-earned break from the often smoky environment in which they lived. In these early years after the end of the war there seemed to be precious little to be cheerful about. Post-war recovery was taking longer than expected to materialise. Clothes rationing had only ended in February 1949 and rationing on some other products existed until July 1954. Later in 1949 the economic problems which had made life difficult in post-war Britain resulted in the Pound being devalued by 30%. No wonder then that the idea of a day *away from it all* was attractive to these local folk!

What better way to spend your Good Friday than to stand in a queue for a charabanc? This was a regular event at the Haymarket in the days before most families had access to a car. The ghostly grey outline of St. Thomas's church is visible on the left of the picture. The building was designed by John Dobson and built in 1830. It stands on the site of an old leper hospital. The Haymarket took its name from its former use as an open market area from which hay and straw was sold. It later became the area from where horse-drawn cabs would ply for trade and it was therefore natural for the area to develop into the place where buses and coaches would congregate in modern days.

NC & J

Above: The unforgettable sight of workers and shoppers queuing for the evening bus home at the Worswick street bus station. This picture was taken in August 1952. The very trusty *Guy* single-decker bus can be seen carefully threading its way past the orderly queue of people. The fashions of the day will create nostalgic thoughts in anyone who was around at the time. The journey home on the bus would have been rather draughtier and noisier than it is today, and of course far fewer people owned cars in the era depicted here.

Top: A relatively tranquil scene featuring the Worswick Street bus station as it appeared in June 1952. Whoever thought up the slogan *Shop at Binns* should be applauded for a) thinking of it and b) *sticking* with it over such a long period of time. Anyone who has studied old photographs or books about the north of England will be familiar with the slogan which seemed to be written on everything capable of movement! The line up of old buses, most of which date from the 1940s rekindles memories of the sights and smells of these sturdy workhorses which clocked up hundreds of thousands of miles during their long periods of service. The sign on the fascia of the enclosed bus station advertises an excursion to the Festival of Britain. Thousands of visitors from the north (and indeed, from all over the world) attended the exhibition which was held on the South Bank of the Thames from May 1951.

Above: A birds-eye view of Newcastle Airport as it appeared in the 1950s. This would be the view seen by passengers as they neared the end of their journey and saw the welcome sight of the large letters spelling out the words NEWCASTLE AIRPORT. During the war the airport was requisitioned by the government and became an R.A.F. base. It reverted to civilian use at the end of the conflict but it was not until 1952 that the commercial side of the operation really began to develop. April 1966 saw the opening of a new runway, and in the following year Harold Wilson had the honour of opening the new terminal building. Increased traffic through the airport resulted in the construction of larger facilities in the 1990s, and the extension and upgrading of the existing terminal building.

Top: This photograph dates from April 1958 and shows traffic heading, albeit very slowly, away from the Tyne Bridge. Work first began on Newcastle's best-known landmark in 1925. The contractors were Dorman Long of Middlesbrough, who were *already* engaged in the construction of the very similar Sydney Harbour bridge in Australia. The final structure contained around 7,000 tons of steelwork and had a main span of 531 ft. The bridge was officially opened on October 10th 1928 by King George V. During the same month this picture was taken British newspapers were full of stories about the birth of a new movement the *Campaign for Nuclear Disarmament*. The pressure group had a simple aim, 'to demand a British initiative to reduce the nuclear peril and to stop the armaments race, if need be by unilateral action by Great Britain'. Over the coming years many marches would be seen around the streets of Newcastle before the campaigners secured their aims.

Above: A rather grim scene recorded in January 1952 at the foot of Pilgrim Street. The cold, grey outline of the Tyne Bridge can just be seen in the distance and a vivid impression of the wintry weather is created by a snow-covered pavement on the left. Typically, the traffic is backed-up towards the Tyne Bridge in one direction - it was often nose-to-tail all the way up to Northumberland Street in the other. Some of these flat-backed lorries may have travelled miles before reaching this point - many without the luxury of a heater in their primitive cabs and some of the drivers would have been concerned about the prospects of a clear run back down the A1 in the winter snow. The problems associated with traffic congestion in this part of Newcastle existed right up until the 1970s when the Central Motorway (East) route opened to speed the flow of traffic through the city.

Below: Congestion on a serious scale was experienced over the *new* Tyne Bridge when this picture was taken in January 1952. The problem was attributed to the closure of the High Level Bridge. All Saints Church can be seen on the left of the picture. Built between 1786-9 on a splendid site overlooking the Tyne, it was designed by David Stephenson. The oval-shaped main part of the church was a rarity, but not enough to prevent the church from being deconsecrated when attendances fell in the 1950s. The building later found use as a teaching resource centre.

Bottom: A contrast between the *old* and the *new* is evident in this picture from 1957. The location of the scene is the junction of Benton Road and the Coast Road. The modern shopping development on the right looks out across the broad, shallow roundabout where a gardener can be seen leaning on his rake and admiring his work. Overhead, the wires for the trolley bus service are visible, supported by the long crooked poles as they hum with the current necessary to power the trolley buses. Notice the motorcycle *combination* approaching the roundabout. The mature rider isn't wearing a helmet - it wasn't a legal requirement in those days.

Below: Newcastle Airport has come a long way since this picture was taken in the mid 1960s! In modern times we take the facility very much for granted - whether for the starting point for an annual holiday or the high flying captain of industry's trips to London and beyond. The airport was only established after a long campaign by local visionaries in the 1930s, convinced of the value of an airport to the growing city. The airport was opened in 1935 by Sir Philip Cunliffe-Lister the government minister responsible for air travel. A new airport terminal was constructed in 1964 and it was probably this that prompted the photographer to take a series of pictures recording the airport before the improvements.

Left: *A busy scene at the Haymarket recorded for us in June 1963. Keen observers may just be able to make out the Haymarket entrance to the Tatler cinema. The main entrance to this sometimes controversial venue was on Northumberland Street. The Tatler News Cinema began life in December 1937 after some years as a popular cafe. The cafe was retained on the upper floor. From the 1950s its main selling point was it specialisation in cartoons as the sign here shows. In 1970 the Tatler became a members-only cinema club. Striptease acts were performed here in the 1970s. After various name changes and attempts to swell audiences the cinema finally closed its doors for the last time in August 1980. The site was later occupied by retailers and a branch of a well-known high street bank.*

Below: *A panoramic view across the Tyne which is dominated by the huge British Courage which takes up half the length of the photograph. Other ships can be seen under construction at the yards along both sides of the river. This picture dates from August 1957 but ship building on a major scale had been carried on here for almost two centuries. Many famous ships have begun life on the banks of this river, among them the Mauretania, launched in 1906 at a ceremony seen by 80,000 people as she slid gracefully down the slipway.*

At work

Bottom: An early start was essential for those trading in fresh fruit and vegetables at the Green Market. One obstacle to this - and one which caused understandable consternation, was the traffic congestion on the narrow streets leading to the area. This picture was taken in July 1955 and the traffic is backed up for over 100 yds - even at 7.45 am! In desperation some of the traders have resorted to unloading produce on the street and wheeling it to the market area, such was the desire to get 'set up' and begin trading.

Below: An early 1950s scene recorded at the Newcastle Cattle Market. It is thought that the picture was taken to mark the end of meat rationing in the years after the end of the war. A note on the back of the original print from which this image is taken states that meat prices *rose* to 10 shillings per hundredweight and predicted that prices would be on the increase for local housewives by the following Monday.

Men at work. Unlike the precautions taken in modern times, these workmen relied only on the protection afforded by some red and white poles and the odd red flag. Pedestrians were left to dodge the rubble as best they could, keeping one eye on the passing traffic as they did so. The scene was set along Northumberland Street in May 1957 and tremendous character is generated by the variety period motor cars - Austin A35s, Vauxhalls with their American styling, and a couple of snub-nosed Ford vans. Many readers will remember shopping trips to the stores shown on the left of the picture - Burtons, H. Samuels, and the ever faithful F.W. Woolworths.

Left: In an unashamed show of unity and force hundreds of striking shipyard workers can be seen marching through the streets of Newcastle on their way to a meeting on a local recreation ground. They are led by a small but effective brass band, playing up-beat tunes to keep their spirits up and show the world that they they were ready for anything. The strikers belonged to the Swan Hunter and Wigham Richardson yards in Wallsend and the picture was taken in March 1957. Some of the more memorable events from the year this picture was taken include the appointment of Harold Macmillan as Prime Minister after Anthony Eden's Suez crisis debacle, the birth of the Common Market with the signing of the Treaty of Rome, the Soviet Union's first steps into space exploration and a fire and subsequent leak of radiation at the *Windscale* nuclear plant in Cumbria. This was the year that saw the deaths of Oliver Hardy and Humphrey Bogart and the time that British holiday makers first discovered the delights of holidays in Benidorm.

Below left: : You could have heard a pin drop in the drawing office of Swan Hunter's when this picture was taken. The date was 1952 and the lads look as if they had not long since left school. The long wooden-trestle drawing boards look rather primitive. Of course this kind of work is nearly all done on the computer screen in modern companies. A job in the drawing office at *Swan's* or any of the other large engineering or ship building companies would have been highly coveted by school leavers. Notice, in this picture, the large weights being used by the apprentice draughtsman on the right. They held a flexible rule in place to enable a long smooth curve to be drawn. Ink was used on the drawings, and each little bottle was tied with string onto a flat wooden square to prevent it from being tipped over or from dripping onto the valuable piece of work.

Bottom: Long before the days of computers, an army of clerical staff was required by every major business in order to keep the wheels of industry turning. The Co-op was no exception - in fact, the nature of the Co-op's organisation probably meant that they needed additional clerical hep in order to keep up with the paperwork. This quite spartan office was situated above the store in Newgate Street. By modern standards the working conditions look a bit on the uncomfortable side with little attention paid to the new science of *ergonomics.* Even the chap in the foreground who appears to hold the position of chief clerk is sat on an uncomfortable bent-wood chair as he works away at his papers.

Left: It may seem crude to the modern eye, but this facility was *state of the art* in the medical word when the picture was taken in March 1958. The location was the premises of Abbott Laboratories and these young ladies were mixing and checking drugs which would eventually find their way into the company's famous pills.

Below left: Even the process of counting and packing the pills at Abbot Laboratories was very labour-intensive. These ladies were preparing bottles for distribution to chemist's shops throughout the land. The photograph was taken in 1958, the year that Elvis Presley began his military service in the U.S.A. and British involvement in Cyprus was causing unrest on the island as civil unrest escalated.
Only weeks before this picture was taken tragedy had struck the world of football when eight Manchester United footballers were among 21 passengers killed in the Munich air crash.

Below: This picture was one in a series of photographs taken for the Co-op in June 1950. The purpose was to promote the enormous retailer as *the place to work* at a time when skilled labour was in short supply. These smart young men are practising their cake decoration skills in the bakery department of the store. The giant retail emporium on Newgate Street had only been open for two decades when this picture was taken. The Co-op had resisted the rush to locate on Northumberland Street that had seemed to grip the rest of the retail world in the 1920s and 1930s. More than a dozen familiar high street names had *staked their claim* on the busy retail axis of Newcastle during that period.

WP

NC & J

Above: Most of the large department stores had a team of skilled people beavering away to produce the internal advertising signs we all take for granted. Examples of their *point of sale material* as the marketing gurus call it, can be seen covering the walls of the tiny office. Messages such as *'After Shopping - Tea at Fenwick's Tea Room'* where customers could enjoy *Willie Walker and the Terrace Tea Room Orchestra.* Some of the signs look very elaborate and colourful; it was a time-consuming job doing all the work by hand in the days before computer graphics and other labour-saving aids. Fenwick's is one of Newcastle's favourite stores. It was founded by John Fenwick who lived between 1846 and 1905. His first shop on Northumberland Street opened in modest premises in 1882, but expansion followed quickly. By 1891 a shop was opened in New Bond Street in London.

Left: It would be impossible not to be impressed by this dramatic photograph. The rows of terraced houses near the shipyard at Wallsend are dwarfed by the breathtaking size of *The World Unicorn* as she nears completion. The contrast between the houses and her monstrous bow is nothing short of incredible. Of course, the children shown here would be used to the sight by the time the giant vessel had reached this stage, and are far more inter-ested in demonstrating their skipping skills for the photographer than gawping at the latest ship to be born on the Tyne.

Sugar and spice and all things nice

Most people have heard of Rowntree & Company, the chocolate and sugar confectioners who were founded by the Rowntree family in York. Henry Rowntree had worked in the Tuke grocery business which was founded as far back as 1725. Rowntree bought the cocoa interests from William Tuke and Sons in 1862 and Joseph Rowntree joined him in 1869.

The company's original business was making cocoa for the beverage Elect Cocoa. Then, in 1880s it began making fruit pastilles and gums. These were a French monopoly at the time but Joseph Rowntree employed Claude Gaget, a French confectioner who came from Paris to York in 1879.

During the 1950s the Rowntree Company, the chocolate and sugar confectioners of York, was having difficulties keeping up with the demand for its products because of labour shortages in the York area.

Meanwhile, in Newcastle upon Tyne, workers were suffering the opposite problem. The forties were not a happy time for them as their town saw a decline in its traditional industries of shipbuilding, heavy engineering and coal mining. In addition, Newcastle women who had worked during the war were looking for alternative employment.

The two problems proved to have a single solution when the Fawdon factory was started in 1956. It took just a year to put up the buildings on a green field site, the Fawdon Industrial Estate, 3½ miles from the centre of

Newcastle. The construction included roads, parking areas and gardens as well as the factory itself. Production commenced in 1957 and the formal opening was in 1958.

The design and building was done by Messrs John Laing & Sons Ltd in consultation with Rowntrees' own architectural and engineering staff. It had a curved roof rising from reinforced concrete valley gutters to north light glazing. In the construction no beams protrude below the curved ceiling. One of the prime objects of the design was the maintenance of high standards of hygiene so essential to a modern food factory.

Top right: Pastilles being manufactured by hand at the Tanner's Moat factory, York, 1890. **Above:** An aerial view of the newly built factory in 1958. **Left:** The attractive gardens to the front of the factory in 1958.

staff were recruited locally. Chocolate was brought from York by tanker. Gelatine came from Germany and Gum Acacia from the Sudan. Milk came from Nestle, Dalston.

Fawdon was served by British Rail with two trains a day on the Ponteland branch. This continued even under the wires of the Tyne and Wear Metro. In fact, until it closed in 1987 it was the only freight service under the wires of the electrified Metro.

With a strong family culture and a vibrant sports and social club, there are many amusing stories particularly in the early days.

In the mid sixties the product range was extended to include the manufacture of Jelly Tots. During this period the factory used temporary staff to cover the

A feature of the site is the landscape garden along the full length of the south side. It includes ornamental pools and rockeries. Together with the banks and cuttings of the Western By-pass at the side of the factory it has been designated a Nature Reserve. The garden was designed by Mr Brian Hackett, a well-known landscape artist and a lecturer on the subject at Durham University.

The site levelling began in August 1955 when it is estimated that over a quarter of a million tons of earth was moved in six weeks. The factory was formally opened on 24th September 1958. An extension to the west end was completed in 1968 and added to in 1977 when extra office space was provided with the completion of a second floor. A sports complex was built for staff in 1978. There is still space remaining on site to build as much again.

When the factory was first opened a handful of managers and supervisors were transferred from York, headed by Mark Jones, but otherwise the 860

Top left: The Lady Mayoress samples the fare on her tour of the factory on opening day, 1958. **Above:** *Members of the Mayoral party chat to staff on opening day.* **Below:** *The packing room.*

Derek Lawrence became factory manager in 1967. The first chocolate production line was installed to produce Mint Cracknell in 1971. Three years later another facility was installed to make Smarties. Mint Cracknell was abandoned in 1978 in favour of Lion Bar manufacture. When Toffee Crisp was introduced, Table Jelly production was transferred to Hadfield.

In 1986 Maurice Goodson took command and Fruit Gum manufacture was brought to Fawdon from York. The factory moved to the modern concept of Teams and Team

Christmas and Easter seasonal packing. At one point, when Matchmakers were being packed by hand the level of permanent and temporary staff rose to 2,000. At Fawdon the year would seem to revolve around seasonal packing programmes, with the accompanying influx of women workers who filled the factory with extra activity and then left the permanent staff in what felt like a state of suspension until the next programme. In the late 1960s, the demand for the new line, Jelly Tots, could could only be met by working a permanent night shift. There was a good response to the request for volunteers and soon they were well established as 'night birds'.

Top left: Packing Selection Boxes for Christmas.
Top right: The gum preparation unit.
Right: Actor Kenneth More during his visit to the factory in 1959. (He started his acting career in Byker!)

Leaders. Rowntree became the Nestle Rowntree Division of Nestle UK Ltd. Towards the end of Mr Goodson's reign, Minties and Tooties were introduced which involved introducing a sugar panning facility.

Roger Darsley managed the factory from 1992 to 1998. During that time the Lion Bar was transferred to a new factory at Dijon, whilst manufacture at Fawdon took on board the wafer line, Blue Riband, and the biscuit line Breakaway. More changes came to Fawdon in 1996 when the Norwich factory closed and £10 million was invested at Fawdon to make Caramac and Rolo, whilst Toffee Crisp was transferred to Castleford. This meant that by 1998 Fawdon had the potential to make 45,000 tonnes of confectionery and had two of Nestle's fourteen International Confectionery Brands, Rolo and Fruit Pastilles.

The present factory manager is Paul Harwood. Currently the Fawdon factory produces half chocolate confectionery and half sugar confectionery, a quarter of which is exported. Chocolate goes to Europe, Canada and Australia. Sugar confectionery goes to Italy and the Middle and Far East, including Australia. Overseas the sugar brands are known as Nestle Fruit Joy or Nestle Frutips. In the UK major supermarkets are the main customers but, as Nestle products are impulse purchases the company likes to have them in every shop, garage and cinema. Everywhere that people are we want our sweets to be.

The company's future plans include the extension of their export markets and the revitalisation of their brands at home. To that end, the factory and stores now operate over 24 hours a day on five days a week, using a two-shift alternating system plus a permanent night shift.

At the reception held in the company dining room to mark the completion of the factory in September 1958, Mr Lloyd Owen, Company Chairman,

reminded staff that they all gained a living in a most competitive industry and expressed the hope that the state of the trade would maintain the new factory in full and successful operation for many years. He would surely agree that his hope has been fulfilled.

Top left: The Fawdon Follies, a Social Club show in 1979. Left: Brendan Foster opens the new wafer plant. Above: The modern Rolo packing facility. Below: The newly refurbished entrance to the factory.

Service to the world's steel industry

To the ordinary man in the street, rolls (the engineering variety) are not very interesting. They appear to be steel cylinders with spindly ends, yet they are perhaps the most vital consumable tool in the production of rolled material which is eventually used by other industries.

The Davy Roll Company was founded in 1970 but to understand how it happened involves going further back. Since the early years of the century the Close Works has been the site of the hot and dirty but highly skilled business of producing iron or steel castings and transforming them into engineering components. Before the mid 1930s it was principally an iron foundry operated by a number of different owners. The basis of its modern activity was established in 1933 when, for the first time, the Close Works became seriously involved in making rolls for rolling steel and other metals. Roll making was also being carried out at the Company's works in Western Road, Jarrow. When Davy Roll was formed this was still an integral part of its operations in the north east. However during the Second World War, the Close Works became involved in the manufacturing armaments and supplying components for Rolls Royce Merlin Engines.

Above: *An early aerial view of Armstrong Whitworth before the old Victorian Terraces had been demolished top make way for high rise flats and modern road links.*
This picture: *Delivery vehicles parked outside the foundry.*

After the war Armstrong Whitworth began to diversify, turning out rock-crushing machinery, anchors and other products. It continued to be a successful firm until the late 1960s when a slow down in general investment began to take its toll. Turnover and profits slumped and a steadily increasing number of workers were made redundant.

For a while it looked as though the Close Works was doomed. Then, in 1968, the massive Davy-Ashmore plant engineering group made a successful takeover bid and began to lay its plans for a totally new roll making operation. This involved cutting out almost all activities except the making of rolls, in line with the parent group's programme of cutting out uneconomic and 'fringe' enterprises.

The Davy Roll Company was formed in 1970 with the merger of four long-established UK roll making companies. They were Armstrong Whitworth Rolls Ltd., Davy and United Roll Foundry Ltd., Brightside Roll Foundry Ltd. and John M. Moorwood Ltd.

Top: *Part of No. 2 bay roll machine shop in 1960*
Left: *Anchors being hoisted aboard ship ready for shipment to the Persian Gulf in 1964.*

It was a vitally important decision that the Davy Roll Company made at its formation in 1970 by turning all its production facilities to roll making. This could have put the company in greater financial troubles than it had suffered in 1968. However, the decision was the right one. The four foundries had their own exclusive expertise. Brought together, they produced a world class roll making facility for producing cast rolls in steel and iron. By 1970, turnover had risen to £3 million, better than in the best years of the old regime.

Work was concentrated in two centres. The North East concerned itself with the really large and heavy rolls, leaving the smaller ones to be made in Sheffield. Instead of looking around for orders for a variety of engineering products, everyone was immersed in making better rolls by improved methods of using more sophisticated marketing techniques.

The parent group's rationalisation programme made available a lot of up-to-date machinery which Davy Roll was able to buy. The whole of the Close Works was to be gutted and revitalised. At the same time, a specialised roll turning

Above: Another aerial view of Armstrong Whitworth in 1965, showing the changing face of Gateshead.
Left: Fettling an alloy steel roll after annealing.

lathe from Germany was bought and a Heat Treatment Furnace was installed for the production of surface hardened back-up rolls.

By the seventies, the company had become the largest manufacturing unit of its kind in Europe and was having an increasing impact on both the British Steel industry and metal production in many other parts of the world. This can be understood when it is realised that about 90% of all steel produced throughout the world passes through a rolling operation at some stage before it reaches the customer.

The Gateshead Division manufactured cast rolls for hot and cold strip mills, medium/heavy section mills and plate mills in a variety of iron and steel qualities.

However in 1978 the Jarrow Works was closed and some of the equipment was transferred to Gateshead. Since then other facilities have been added at the Gateshead foundry, including melting furnaces, drying stoves, vertical spin casting machines built by Davy International in Sheffield, cranes and heat treatment furnaces. The machine shop has gained three new specialist CNC machines, a Hoesch MFD twin saddle heavy duty

Above: Tapping a 15 ton air furnace. **Right:** *Setting up chills for chill rolls.*

roughing and finishing lathe, a Geminis single saddle CNC lathe and a Waldrich CNC twin miller, the first of its kind in the world!

Presently being installed is a large lathe for back-up rolls and heavy steel rolls and retrofits of older lathes, grinders and millers. These machines easily achieve the high tolerances required for modern rolling mill rolls.

The Davy Roll company carries out a comprehensive series of inspection tests during the manufacturing cycle of the rolls. To improve the tests it has invested in a spectrographic analyser, several ultrasonic testing machines, Equotip hardness testing machines, residual stress measurement equipment and a spark erosion machine. These devices complemented the fine equipment already being used in the Inspection and Metallurgical Laboratory.

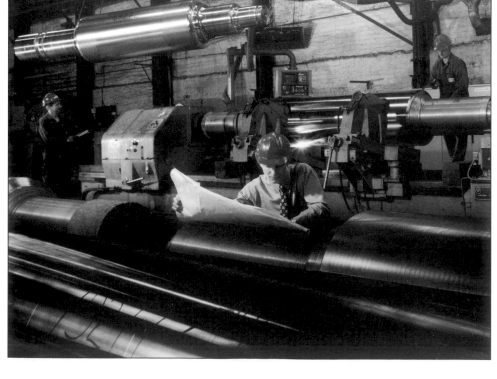

The company is dedicated to achieving continual improvements in the quality and service offered to its customers. In 1992 the Gateshead Works was awarded independent accreditation to the Quality Management System ISO 9002/1987. Two years later, further accreditation to BS EN ISO 9002/1994 was obtained, Davy Roll Company, Gateshead, being

Above: A Spin Casting Machine. Left: Machining Work Rolls.

manufacturers and assemblers in the world...' As members of Kvaerner, the wide-ranging expertise of its sister companies in the design and operation of mills is available to Davy Roll.

The Davy Roll Company's interest in the rolls produced does not stop once they are delivered. A team of technicians with wide experience of mill applications is available to advise on all aspects of roll use. Technical support is further extended by a mobile metallurgical inspector who can inspect and maintain rolls in service.

Top left: Grinding a Plate Mill Roll. *Below:* A modern aerial view of the Davy Roll premises in Gateshead.

the first roll maker in the world to achieve the new 1994 standard. The Gateshead Company has also been awarded the VDEh accreditation in 1995. This organisation represents many steel makers in Europe and the VDEh is a very prestigious award.

Gateshead runs a Total Quality Involvement Programme which has been developed over the last three years and which involves all the personnel within the works. It has a partnership agreement with Hoogovens of the Netherlands which has been in existence since 1995 and there have been substantial mutual benefits. Partnership Agreements have been discussed and implemented with British Steel and are being assessed with several companies throughout the world. Several agreements will be concluded in the near future.

The areas of current research work are in new production techniques, solidification modelling and further development of well established roll materials by alloying and heat treatment. New roll sleeve materials are being investigated for producing better rolled products.

In 1996 Davy Roll was taken over by the Kvaerner Group which justly describes itself as world leaders in the design, engineering and construction facilities...Suppliers to steel and aluminium producers of cost effective, reliable, high-performance equipment...One of the most sophisticated

Pickling to perfection

It all began in Newcastle back in 1918. The First World War had just come to an end, leaving a number of goods in short supply. One of them was vinegar.

James Robertson Ross was not one to miss an opportunity. Having been invalided out of the Royal Engineers, with an Army gratuity and a horse, he made his own brand of the valuable liquid, then added pickles to the vinegar. His fish and chip shop had closed whilst he was away at the war, and so he and his wife Elizabeth began by selling pickles to public houses and clubs in Byker, Newcastle, which were then given away free to customers. From their Raby Street home Elizabeth peeled and pickled and, apart from the clubs, James sold from a horse and cart.

The business went up in the world. In 1922 the cart was redundant and deliveries were made by James' first T Ford lorry. When the taste of his pickles became well known, he progressed to selling them from a market stall.
His pickles were packed into stone jars and sold loose. Later, a Sunderland glass firm introduced half-gallon jars and this gave Mr Ross the idea of packing the pickles in glass, immersed in light-coloured vinegar, thus improving their 'image'
In 1928 there was a move to Byker Bank, then, in 1936 there was another move, this time to Elswick Station, Scotswood Road. In the same year a £100 Private Limited Company was formed. In time the business was handed down to James' and Elizabeth's son Cecil and his wife Emily. The firm had a reputation for being meticulous in their handling of food.
Emily, a house-proud North country wife insisted on the same high standards in the factory as in her kitchen.

After completing their National Service, Cecil's and Emily's three sons, Gordon, Tommy and James entered the firm. Each of them

Above: Cecil Ross, the founders' son who took control of the firm in 1936.
Below: Staff packing and labelling assorted pickles.
*Right: Gordon Ross, the founders grandson at a food exhibition. **Facing page top:** An early advert for Ross's Pickles.*

contributed his special talents to the success of the company.

James travelled the world searching for equipment for the new factory. In fact the Dilute Brine-maker was his own invention which was patented and put on the market. Tommy, who was formerly a chef, was able to bring his own expertise into the quality, flavouring and general production of the pickles. Gordon was the sales

director, regularly travelling abroad to obtain export orders. In addition, he obtained, unsought, a pile of letters

Proved by POPULAR DEMAND

Ross's

The PICK of PICKLES

AS ADVERTISED ON TV

Ross's PICKLED ONIONS

Obtainable from all good Grocers and Stores

Phone 34360   JAMES ROSS & SON (NEWCASTLE) LTD
CAMBRIDGE PRESERVING WORKS,
NEWCASTLE UPON TYNE, 4.

from Kuwait, Holland, Norway and Malta, testifying to the quality of the firm's pickling processes.

At this point no-one had been able to perfect a machine to take off onion skins. They had to be peeled by hand and girls were employed every day doing just that. Fortunately they soon became used to the irritation caused to the ordinary housewife doing this task and so none of them spent the day in tears once they had been on the job for a short while.

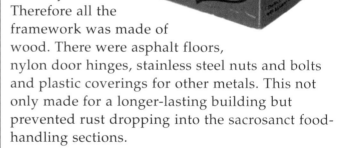

By the early sixties the company directors were looking for a site where further growth could take place without the necessity for more moves. The prefect one presented itself on the Newburn Trading Estate, with three and a half acres of land. Mrs Elizabeth Ross, at the age of 89 was still taking an active interest in the business. She laid the foundation

Top left: Elizabeth Ross at the age of 89, preparing to lay the foundation stone for the new factory at Newburn in 1965. Top right: A point-of-sale display unit for Ross's Pickles. Above: Another early advert for Ross. Right: The pickling room where the vegetables are soaked in brine prior to bottling.

stone of the new factory at Newburn with a speech that reminded her audience that, although the firm currently handled 600 bags of onions a day, she and her husband began with just half a bag. The new factory was a triumph for the modern pickling industry and was referred to by the handbook of the Food Manufacturers' Federation as the best of its type.

The pickling industry uses organic acids which make its premises more vulnerable to corrosion than those of any other branch of the food industry. Therefore all the framework was made of wood. There were asphalt floors, nylon door hinges, stainless steel nuts and bolts and plastic coverings for other metals. This not only made for a longer-lasting building but prevented rust dropping into the sacrosanct food-handling sections.

The firm was processing up to 40 tons of onions (from Holland, Egypt, Poland, Italy and the UK) each week. Baby beets were introduced at this time as a new line. They are grown in the early part of the year and then processed, like fruit, while they are young and fresh.

A dock strike round about this time meant no imported onions. Hectic phone calls resulted in

their fleet of vans driving south to various farms, picking up ten bags here and ten bags there, in competition with every other pickling firm in the country. They managed to keep their staff fully employed and to keep up the traditional service to their customers.

In 1972, Gordon, James and Tommy Ross, with their mother Emily, went to Holland to test a new packing machine for their factory. They took their own onions in their hand luggage -which had been imported from Holland! This puzzled the customs officers considerably. The machine pleased them, so they had it installed at Newburn.

The fourth generation of the Ross family is today actively involved in senior management positions. The company is still one of the few which peels its own onions, though by machine these days. Modern technology is used throughout the plant, but used in production of the old traditional recipes.

Many workers have been with the company for many years and allied to the family provide the continuity essential for further expansion.

Recent expansion has included a new canteen block and additional floor area for vinegar and vegetable preparation. Growth is continually financed from the reinvestment of profits. Environmental issues are very much to the forefront in planning and James Ross and Son have installed a new drainage and effluent treatment plant. It all adds up to a recipe for success.

Top: A line drawing of the Newburn factory, when newly built, it has since undergone four phases of expansion and there is still room for further expansion if necessary.
Bottom left: Checking the quantity of pickles in the jars.
Below: A selection of pickles born out of 80 years of pickling experience and family tradition.

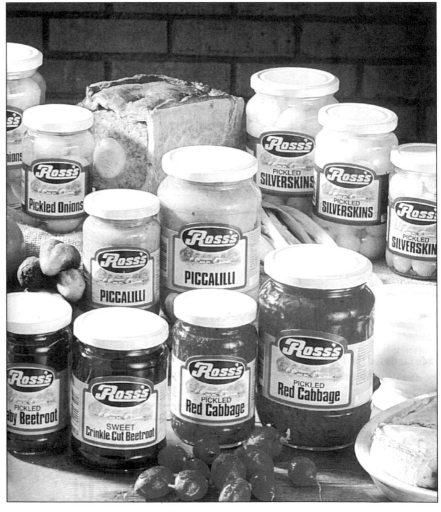

A reflection on water

The 1980s were declared the 'Decade of Water' by the United Nations' as they realised that water is an increasingly rare and threatened resource. At the same time it is the most vital element in humanity's long fight for survival. We can survive three weeks without food but, after three days without water, we die.

England's first Public Health Act was not introduced until 1848. When it came it was the direct result of a wave of epidemic diseases, principally cholera which scared society into the beginnings of sanitation. However, another half century passed before it was realised that public health would continue to deteriorate unless something was done about the sanitary conditions in the country's huge areas of industrial slums. The act compelled the provision of a constant piped supply of water, with proper sewage and sanitary facilities to prevent contamination of supplies. Any wastage or fouling of water was punishable by law.

Newcastle and Gateshead Water Company
William Yarnold's Waterworks had provided some sort of water supply for Newcastle and Gateshead from 1697. It was succeeded in the latter year by Ralph Lodge's Waterworks, which in turn was taken over by the Newcastle Fire Office in 1797. The Fire Office, together with the Subscription Water

Unfortunately reservoirs leaked from fissures in the embankments which proved to be due to subsidence. Putting matters right added considerably to the original cost but it enabled the company to supply 370,000 consumers with 35 gallons of water each a day.

No new water provision is sufficient for very long. The population increases and the standard of living rises. When it was decided to build the Catcleugh Reservoir, Bateman was rejected in favour of Thomas Hawksley but there were still quarrels about paying for it that reverberated into the new century.

An aerial ropeway 600 yards long, crossing the Tyne

Company, formed in the first part of the new century, set up the Newcastle and Gateshead Water Company in 1863.

This water company, one of the first in England, obtained as its chairman Richard Burdon Sanderson, a gentleman of leisure who had time to attend to its interests. A reservoir was constructed at Hallington using the services of a Mr Bateman, an eminent engineer whose price was high and somewhat resented by the water company directors. The directors were doubtless further displeased when Sanderson reduced their own fees.

He also attacked the problem of waste through leakage which was losing about a sixth of the company's production. The disastrous consequences of a fire which could not be put out for lack of water led him to suggest that the local authority should establish a fire brigade. It was made up of insurance personnel and policemen and headed by a chief constable who was paid £20 a year.

New reservoirs

Towards the end of the century, concerned about the area's high death rate, the Newcastle Authority considered running the water undertaking itself but decided against it. There was a great deal of criticism, both local and governmental, of the service and various improvement schemes were suggested. Eventually, a site at Colt Crag was decided on for a new reservoir., with another at Swinburn. A narrow - gauge railway had to be built to carry materials to the site. The services of the unfortunate Mr Bateman were called upon again.

*Above: The Rede Pipeline between Catcleugh and Whittle Dene in 1895. **Below:** The Pilgrim Street premises built in 1897. **Facing page, top:** Opening day at Benwell pumping station in 1903. **Facing page, bottom:** A fire brigade tender from 1868, built at the suggestion of the water company.*

Metropolitan Water Board with repairs to mains in London. Stanley George Barrett was appointed engineer in 1941 and, by the next year there were notices in the local press asking for economical use of water. Towards the end of the war, in 1944, came the Rural Water Supply and Sewerage Act which set £15 million aside for rural water supply. Having reached out from its original statutory area to the surrounding boroughs, over the years, the Newcastle and Gateshead Water Company took this opportunity to meet the demands of rural districts of Northumberland. Between 1950 and 1963 the Newcastle company acquired the undertakings of the Castle Ward, Bellingham, and nine other rural district councils. Meanwhile, also in 1950 there began a construction plan which achieved the provision of 64 service reservoirs and six treatment works for the supplying of water to the rural area.

1952 brought the formation of the Coquet Water Board, with its River Coquet scheme in 1959.

In 1982 the Northumbrian Water Authority completed the construction of the Kielder Reservoir.

from Wylam to Prudhoe, and connected to a branch of the NE railway, transported 20 tons of sand a day for the construction of new filters at Whittle Dean in 1900. The Rede pipeline between Catcleugh and Whittle Dene was brought into use in 1895. It was 30 inches in diameter and 27 miles long. Catcleugh Reservoir was stocked with fish and an angling club was formed.

The wars

During the first world war the development of Armstrong's armament factory caused water consumption to rise and so the Wylam pumping station was reopened and converted to electricity.

Electrification followed at Gateshead, Benwell and Barrasford in the twenties and thirties. In 1939 the waterworks were guarded by Home Guard Units and the following year some of the staff were seconded to help the

people in the North East of England.

Water Quality

The Newcastle company had long been concerned about leakage and pollution of supplies. After the initial filter work at Whittle Dean, new plant has been supplied there in 1939 as well a major new filtration system that was finished in 1992.

Suez Lyonnaise des Eaux

This French company concerned itself with the administration of both water and energy sources until 1980 when Jerome Monod became its president in 1980. He embarked on an ambitious programme of international development, which included a partnership with the Newcastle and Gateshead Water Company in 1988. Four years later, this company amalgamated with Sunderland and South Shields PLC to form North East Water.

Northumbrian Water

A further change in name took place in 1996 when Lyonnaise merged North East Water with Northumbrian Water to create a company which supplies water and sewerage services to 2.6 million

After government legislation the company was quick to install the Paterson chlorine plant in 1926. Henderson filters were installed at Throckley in 1956 and the Warkworth filtration work (River Coquet Scheme) five years later.

As a result of the Kielder scheme Newcastle built the Ovingham pumping station and Horsley treatment Works on the River Tyne.

Water Aid

Water Aid is the charity of the British water industry. Founded in 1981, it raises funds to finance projects in Africa and Asia. It acts as a catalyst to help local communities to help themselves in water and sanitation schemes.

Today, 1.4 billion people still lack access to safe water and 2 billion lack access to adequate sanitation, which puts the activities of the companies in the North East in the past into perspective.

Above and left: The opening of the new filtration works at Whittle Dene in May 1992 by HRH The Princess Royal.
Facing page, top: This instrument was installed at Whittle Dene to control the flow of water. No longer in use, it is the last one in existence in the UK. Facing page, bottom: Catcleugh Reservoir.

Stephenson Clarke - 'These splendid ships...'

Stephenson Clarke Shipping Ltd is the oldest British shipping company but finds itself in the late nineties in a business as vital to the nation's economy as when it began. It tells the remarkable story of a relationship between two great cities, London and Newcastle and the trade between them that made them feel like neighbours despite being separated by 350 miles of dangerous sea

It was 1730 when brothers Ralph and Robert Clarke purchased an interest in a 300-ton sailing vessel and their limited trading activities were to develop during the next 275 years into the present shipowning and ship management business.

Sons of a Long Benton vicar, they took up seafaring careers and became master mariners. By buying shares in ships, they gradually established themselves as ship owners, although they continued to serve at sea for some time. In Robert's hands the business all but collapsed in the middle of the 19th century but better times came again.

Robert Clarke had two sons, John and Ralph. John married Jane Stephenson and moved to London to set up business with his brother, Ralph, carrying on the business of shipowners and coal factors and in this way the foundations of the present shipping company were laid.

The company was built on the coal trades from north east England to the Thames providing coal for domestic heating and industrial use. The coal was often traded as well as transported. The brothers also represented their father's and uncle's business in the capital.

When John Clarke died in 1792, his wife took his place in the business and four years after she retired, Ralph took a new partner, J. Burgess. John and Jane had two sons, Robert and Stephenson. Robert (the eldest) joined the firm in 1806 and when he died aged 67 it fell to the younger son, Stephenson, who was already in the business, to take over. Stephenson Clarke & Company was formed the following year.

In 1865 the first recorded steamers, 'M E Clarke', 'C S Butler' and 'J M Strachan' were built by Palmers of Jarrow for the company. Five years later, Stephenson Clarke signed a contract to carry 15,200 tons of coal to Southampton Gasworks in monthly quantities varying between 800 and 2,400 tons. For almost 100 years the company's ships supplied the Southampton Works until carbonisation ceased in 1968.

After the First World War

The ten years that followed the first war were difficult ones for Stephenson Clarke but the time was used to consolidate the business. With the formation of the Normandy Shipping Company in 1915 came the first working association with the Powell Duffryn Steam Coal Company. This was strengthened in 1921 by the formation of Maris Export & Trading Company. Powell Duffryn Steam Coal and Stephenson Clarke were the partners and the share capital was £250,000.

Above left: Robert Clarke who founded the company with his brother, Ralph.
Left (both pictures): The interior of an early twentieth century ship.

Maris was created to deal with the export activities of both businesses, dealing in coke, pitch and patent fuels. The fleet was built up by the addition of the Vaux, the Cranford and the Lys so that by 1920, 7.8 million tons of coal was being delivered by sea.

In 1928, Colonel Stephenson Clarke retired and Sir Stephenson Kent became chairman. The existing company went into voluntary liquidation and a new company was formed.

For much of the twenties and thirties life on a steam collier remained as it had been for years. The journey from Newcastle to London still took about 30 hours at an average of 9 knots. The crews had to wait for the tides. Only a couple of ships could make Garrison Point by second tide but all of them arrived by the third. This fact led to the ships being known as 'three leggers'. It was extremely hard work battening down the wooden hatches. Known as 'dominoes', there could be up to 120 of them and each had to be separately lifted off and stacked away. Later came steel hatch covers which cut this task from a freezing three quarters of an hour to less than three minutes.

Other changes made life on board more comfortable for the men. Bedding was put on board instead of 'Donkeys' Breakfasts', which was the crew's name for the straw mattresses they stuffed themselves.

The Steyning, built for the company at Clelands Shipbuilding co. Ltd. of Wallsend on Tyne in 1983 and still trading within the fleet.

The Birling, built in 1977 for Stephensons by Clelands Shipbuilding Company Ltd of Wallsend-on-Tyne. This picture shows her launch.

It was a hard life but, in the depression of the thirties these men were working when millions were unemployed.

1939-45
In 1939 the company had its own fleet of 19 vessels. Only three survived the war intact. 'Borde' was lost to requisitioning by the Admiralty. She was fitted out to become the world's first electromagnetic Mine Destructor Vessel, detonating her first mine on Christmas Eve that first year. In the process, the crew had to stand on rubber mats to avoid getting broken ankles from the shock waves.

Apart from the danger of attack, marine hazards included the removal of navigation lights and the need to avoid making smoke. The good firemen

stoked little and often so there was less smoke for the enemy to see.

Broadhurst was the first Stephenson Clarke vessel to be torpedoed by a fast and lethal German E-boat. The east coast was particularly prone to this danger and became known as 'E-boat alley'

The 111 men killed were part of the terrible price paid by the seamen of Shields. The area lost more seafaring men in the second war than any other place in the world.

Stephenson Clarke- pioneers once more
At the end of the war, the company fleet consisted of eleven vessels. It was built up by the acquisition of a number of new ships, notably the Seaford 2.

Company was acquired by the International Maritime Group in September 1997. IMG has now moved its headquarters to Newcastle and so has created a major maritime corporation in the area, re-inforcing the North East's rightful position as an important centre for maritime business.

At 1,500 deadweight tons she was the first of many purpose-built, diesel-engined colliers. Crew facilities included private cabins, showers and laundries.

The increased fleet reflected the growth of the power industries. In early 1950 Stephenson Clarke began to manage hopper barges to dispose of waste at sea. The changing needs of electric power stations led in 1957 to the acquisition of the company's first oil tankers and the renowned 'Flatirons', which were colliers especially built with a low wheelhouse to pass under the London Bridges to deliver coal directly to the upriver powerstations.

The most innovative development of this period was the result of the gas industry's search for ways of transporting natural gas to supplement coal. Stephenson Clarke bought an American wartime motor ship for this purpose. Re-equipped, she became the 'Methane Pioneer' and in 1959 she was the first ship to transport methane across the high seas.

In the sixties North Sea Gas became a real threat to the coal trade. Therefore, in 1970 Stephenson Clarke bought some of the vessels operated for the Gas Board. Once again the company had adapted to the threats from progress and technology. It seemed a good time for a change of name to reflect its pre-eminent role as a shipping company. It became Stephenson Clarke Shipping Limited. During the 70s and 80s the company continued to expand its fleet both in size of ship and in number owned. Having become independent in 1992 through a management buy-out, the

Today, Stephenson Clarke encompasses a range and size of vessel, trading throughout Europe with a highly diverse range of goods that to the original Clarke brothers would have been as inconceivable as putting a man on the moon. However, they would still appreciate the dedicated seamanship of the men and the unending importance of that humble mineral that started it all - coal from Newcastle.

Above: Washington - this ship carries 8,600 tons of cargo and was built in 1977 by Kagoshima Dock & Iron Works Co Ltd, Kagoshima.
Below: The Ashington built in 1979 by Swan Hunter Shipbuilders Ltd, Wallsend & Neptune yards, Tyne.

F H Thompson & Sons Limited
Wood - you like to know

100 Years
-1897-   -1997-

The start of the business can be traced back to a receipt for 10 shillings, issued for office furniture sold by Ralph Thompson to his son Frederick Harrison dated October 1897. His office was at Sandhill, near the quayside where the firm traded from until 1927. His business was mainly in hardwoods for the many furniture manufacturers in the area, but, as business flourished, he traded also in glassware and marble slabs and he took on a lubricating oil agency.

At the end of the First World War the fashion for marble furnishings declined as plywood became available. The firm were one of the first importers of plywood to the UK, distributing throughout the North, from cargoes arriving into the Tyne from Scandinavia.

1927 brought a move from Sandhill to Skinnerburn Road, establishing the offices alongside the yard and so providing more centralised organisation.

Gradually the firm's range of products expanded to include Sundeala and Venesta specialist plywoods, a new section was also started in hardwood flooring contracting.

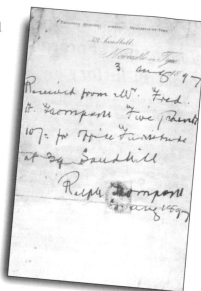

The firm completed several large flooring contracts including the Newcastle Co-operative premises in Waterloo Street. In 1935 an office was opened in Leeds to exploit the potential in the Yorkshire area, with some success in the early years.

During the Second World War the company acted as stockists for the Government, controlling dispersal sites throughout the North of England, supplying license holders authorised by the Government with timber and plywood.

Besides its trade in wood, the company had become local distributors of Formica in February 1955.

Above: The receipt from the start of the business.
Below: The warehouse at 26 Sandhill. F. H. Thompson's eldest son Jack is pictured standing beside the delivery vehicle, complete with human starter, solid rubber tyres and oil lamps.

A new Board of Directors was established by the Company's current chairman and in the following year the current commercial director started his career. The business was duly reorganised resulting in the closure of the Yorkshire office in Leeds.

Accounts produced to March 1959 showed a trading profit for the first time in a number of years. At this time an offer for the company was received from a National Merchant and rejected as unsatisfactory.

Trading was improving with several notable hardwood flooring contracts completed at this time. The two largest being 29,000 sq. yards at Durham County Council offices at Aykley Heads and the Stephenson Building, chemistry and fine art departments at Newcastle University.

Formica continued to increase in popularity, with trade increasing within the DIY sector. A cut to size service was especially well used. In addition trade users were increasingly interested and volumes improved steadily over this period.

This plastic surfacing material from America had become popular and the Company soon became experts in its many and varied uses. As local agents for Richard Graefe, high quality veneered panelling was supplied, much of it to the merchant vessels being built in the shipyards of Tyneside, Wearside and Teesside.

One notable hardwood floor refurbished by the firm was at Harewood House, the home of the then Princess Royal.

In 1957 the partnership became a limited company under the title F. H. Thompson & Sons Limited. The annual accounts of the company to March 1957 were 12 months overdue and when they were finally produced the company was at a very low ebb. All the principals in the partnership had died during the period 1951 to 1958 and this had a detrimental effect on trading.

Top: The company founder Frederick Harrison Thompson.
Right: The stock and price list from October 1937.

During the early sixties the hardwood shed blew down in the south yard and the stock had to be covered with tarpaulins. Investigations into the rebuilding of this showed that it was not viable because of building regulations. The lease on the premises from Edward & James Richardson was due for renewal in two years and as landlords they were not prepared to

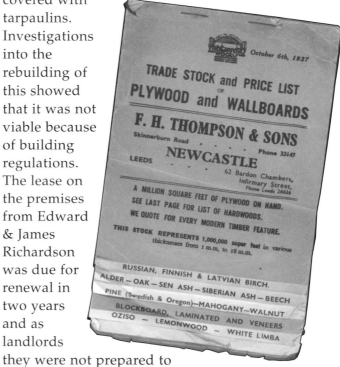

October 6th, 1937

TRADE STOCK and PRICE LIST
OF
PLYWOOD and WALLBOARDS

F. H. THOMPSON & SONS
Skinnerburn Road
NEWCASTLE   Phone 33147
LEEDS   62 Bardon Chambers,
Infirmary Street.
Phone Leeds 26636

A MILLION SQUARE FEET OF PLYWOOD ON HAND.
SEE LAST PAGE FOR LIST OF HARDWOODS.
WE QUOTE FOR EVERY MODERN TIMBER FEATURE.

THIS STOCK REPRESENTS 1,000,000 super feet in various
thicknesses from 1 m.m. to 18 m.m.

RUSSIAN, FINNISH & LATVIAN BIRCH.
ALDER — OAK — SEN ASH — SIBERIAN ASH — BEECH
PINE (Swedish & Oregon)—MAHOGANY—WALNUT
BLOCKBOARD, LAMINATED AND VENEERS
OZISO — LEMONWOOD — WHITE LIMBA

spend any money on the existing buildings. Everything on the site was in a poor state of repair and the company started to look for new premises. It considered plans, first to erect second hand steel aircraft hangars on an available site in Skinnerburn Road, and then to lease a warehouse in Newburn, but neither scheme proved practicable.

Eventually it was decided to lease a site south of the river. Consisting of 1.75 acres, it belonged to

Felling Urban District Council and was offered at a rental of £750 a year. The Yorkshire Insurance Company, for whom Thompsons had been agents for many years, provided finance for a warehouse and offices and a lease agreement was drawn up with rent reviews every seven years.

George H Gray & Partners architects were commissioned to draw up plans for a proposed building encompassing warehouse offices and fabrication facilities. The original design was refused due to the pitch on the roof being too great. After a reduction to 15 degrees this was passed. It was later discovered it is difficult to maintain a waterproof roof of this design.

Above: A vessel at the Skinnerburn Road jetty delivering goods to F H Thompson and Sons. **Left and facing page:** *Two pictures taken in 1949 showing some of F H Thompson and Sons fleet of delivery vehicles and storage areas at Skinnerburn Road.*

The building was completed in September 1967 and all male staff worked every day for six weeks before the move. The move to Felling enabled the firm to have better handling equipment including a Lansing Bagnall reach truck. This was important as sheet materials were being packed in minimum one-ton pallets for efficient handling by forklift or crane. There was now space for an increased stock of sheet materials and also for some new lines for distribution. The hardwood stock was brought from Skinnerburn Road but difficulties in handling hardwood with the new reach trucks led to cessation of hardwood trading.

Sales increased from £450,000 in 1968 to £678,000 in 1972 with profit in the same period rising from £19,000 to £32,000. The company had been trading in Formica laminate for some years and were appointed as Main Distributors in 1960 purchasing direct from Formica. An increasing part of sales growth was due to the service provided by the fabrication unit, involving cutting of sheet materials and bonding Formica to provide work surfaces to order. In 1972, the warehouse had become obviously too small. Its original design had allowed for a 50% extension to be easily constructed and this work was done. At the same time the fabrication shop and the offices were extended, the Yorkshire Insurance Company again helping with financial arrange-ments. This new space allowed the company to stock some new products including ceiling materials and doors.

> **"THE FIRE BURNED FOR SOME TIME BEFORE A PASSING POLICEMAN NOTICED THE GLOW AND ALERTED THE FIRE BRIGADE"**

The company suffered an arson attack in the summer of 1972. The fire burned for some time before a passing policeman noticed the glow and alerted the fire brigade. The fire, however, had been confined to one room, thanks to its Danum Incombustible ceiling which saved the whole building from destruction. Unfortunately, the receipt for the original furniture with which the founder had established his business was destroyed when the desk which contained it was burned to ashes.

This picture: H.R.H. Queen Elizabeth the Queen Mother with Jack Thompson at the Royal Agricultural Show on the Town Moor, Newcastle upon Tyne where the company was an exhibitor in 1956. This was prior to the show's move to its new permanent home in Warwickshire.

In the same year it was decided to dispose of the flooring part of the business as profits had fluctuated for a while and the finance could be better used to update the distribution side of the business. The flooring side of the business was bought by one of the company's long serving joiners Hedley Adamson.

In 1974 the Yorkshire Insurance Company offered to sell the Felling premises to the company. The price agreed was £150,000, which was considered a good investment since a substantial increase in rent was expected at the seven-year rent review.

In 1978 the Company set up a distributorship for Di Lusso flat pack kitchens. This market was

expanding rapidly where distributors held stock to service a number of kitchen centres, who sold from displays only. This partnership operated successfully for three years before Di Lusso were sold to a direct seller and distribution finished.

Until the early eighties, all sales invoices had been typed by hand, with sales analysis and debtors ledgers being updated manually. For a while the Company tried using slightly more sophisticated Olivetti machines but soon they became involved with ICL who recommended a computer programmer, David Berg. Mr Berg wrote bespoke programmes for them for five years.

A completely new computer system was introduced in 1996, incorporating up to date technology and providing better availability of information.

When the business of George L Lockey came up for sale in 1984, the company felt that it offered an ideal opportunity to expand, by increasing sales of complimentary products of softwood and hardwood to its existing customers. The business was purchased, updated with new machinery and sales expanded into new products and markets. 1987 brought re-organisation and a plan to set up a subsidiary company to manufacture laminated plastic panels. Encouraged by Formica Ltd. Thompsons found premises on Victoria Industrial Estate, Hebburn, with an existing factory of 10,000 square feet. Laminform opened in May 1988 with a workforce of six skilled operatives and a factory supervisor, which was soon increased to twelve.

In 1988 trading was buoyant and the factory was extended to allow for increased production. During the building work the original factory was set alight by welders, causing significant damage. Work was completed in September 1990

coinciding with the onset of the recession, resulting in the Company operating below capacity for a number of years.

The trading climate for F H Thompson is now as competitive as it has ever been and the company continues to explore new methods of trading such as the Internet and new products as they become available. Employees continue to play a major part in the success of the company, with six completing over 30 years of service and many more following close behind.

The business is now run by the fourth generation of the founding family and remains committed to wood as a product and the principles of quality and service that have successfully guided it over the past 100 years. Wood, a truly natural product with inherent variety and beauty is environmentally friendly. With correct specification, design and maintenance, satisfactory performance over many decades can be achieved from this unique building material.

Below: An interior view of some of the storage at the Felling site.

A century and a half of local printing pride

The founder of what is now the Ward Philipson Group was Robert Ward, who, early in 1845, decided to go to London to examine the prospects for the printing industry. They obviously impressed him and, being always a man who got on with the job, he was in business by the end of the year, with premises, machinery and staff all ready.

The original factory was in St Nicholas' Cathedral Yard in Newcastle, immediately next door to the workshop of a relative by marriage, Thomas Bewick the world famous wood engraver.

Bewick himself had died but his son ran a business turning out engraved wooden blocks for illustrations, all of which required printing.

Business flourished for Wards as Robert constantly watched the printing market to see where the gaps were. He spotted the need for a business directory. He produced the first Wards' Directory of Newcastle upon Tyne in 1850. From then it was published annually for almost 100 years, until being sold to one of the publishing giants in 1948.

In 1853 Robert Ward embarked on another new venture, the publication of the first Half-penny newspaper ever published in the United Kingdom, the North of England Advertiser. This provided work for the factory and considerable good publicity for the business. Clearly Robert Ward was a very capable businessman and his company was growing remarkably fast.

A new prosperity

The prosperity of the area in general and the firm in particular was given a welcome extra boost when the River Tyne was dredged and widened. This process had begun as far back as 1838 but it took 24 years' work before big ships could be built upstream. They could also be loaded upstream, in fact as far up as Newcastle itself. This was bad news for the Keelmen who had ferried coal downstream to the colliers who were waiting for it but for Tyneside there was an economic surge and Newcastle became one of the most prosperous places in the country, possibly in the world. Eighteen million tons of coal were

exported annually, a hundred ships were built every year and iron ore at Consett meant steel making for ship building on the doorstep where coal fired the furnaces.

The next generation

Robert Ward took full advantage of all this economic activity. In spite of having taken over Bewick's workshop, his factory had become far too small. It was decided to build a new factory to Wards' own specifications at the bottom of Dean Street. The business continued there until Robert died, leaving the firm in the capable hands of two of his sons.

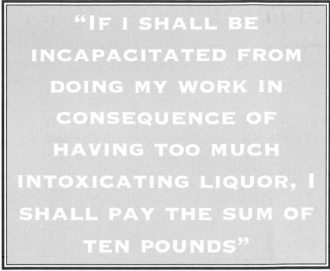

"IF I SHALL BE INCAPACITATED FROM DOING MY WORK IN CONSEQUENCE OF HAVING TOO MUCH INTOXICATING LIQUOR, I SHALL PAY THE SUM OF TEN POUNDS"

However, one of the brothers liked a drink or two, leaving the responsibility for the firm to the other. Ernest Bewick Ward became so angry at the antics of his younger brother that an affidavit to restrain him was drawn up which still exists today. It began, "If I shall be incapacitated from doing my work in consequence of having taken too much intoxicating liquor, I shall pay the sum of ten pounds." This action obviously had the desired effect since the business continued to run successfully.

Another move

The widening of the Dean Street viaduct carrying the railway meant that the business

had to move again, this time to High Bridge, 'high' referring to the upper bridge which used to cross the river running beneath what is now Grey Street. The premises were substantial, occupying a site of 1,500 square yards. Here, the business survived two world wars, together with the intervening slump and general strike, an international paper shortage, a three month national printing strike and the machinations of a string of different Chancellors of the Exchequer.

In the thirties, Ernest Bewick Ward handed over to son Leslie, who, in turn was succeeded by fourth generation John in the sixties who was later joined by Robin.

Rapid and radical changes

Over the preceding 120 years technology had advanced at a very easy pace, although many small improvements and refinements had continually been made. Printing was still mainly a mechanical process using metal type.

Right: A gathering of staff for the company's 75th Anniversary. Centre: An end view of the composing room, 1904. Top: Ernest Bewick Ward who ran the business, along with his brother from 1833. Facing page top left: The founder, Robert Ward. Facing page, top right: An original parcel label from around 1845, depicting the cathedral and the City coat of arms. Facing page, bottom: A beautifully detailed letterhead created to show the move to the new premises in High Bridge in 1902.

entrance with several businesses was far from ideal and Wards became tired of sending politely worded requests to a brewer's drayman to move his wagon, especially when they were ignored.

Purpose built premises

The move to Dunston in 1971 got rid of all the inconvenience. The new premises were purpose-built and single storey with easy access. A lot of money had been spent on new litho plant as well as the building. It was therefore a great disappointment that the country entered the worst recession since the slump of the 30s, exacerbated by 27% inflation and the miners' strike and subsequent 3 day week.

In their usual fashion Wards weathered the storm by a combination of hard work and clever management. In 1973 the company was joined by John Moreels, the first ever director appointed outside the family. Heavy investment in multi colour presses resulted in a blue-chip customer list and a determination to stay ahead of competition by further investment.

Retail outlets and acquisitions

As Newcastle had developed, so had the graphics and artists' material industry. Clients for whom Wards were already doing printing began to buy the pre-printing materials and so Wards Art & Crafts (formerly Graphics) became one of the largest stockists of products from many international companies. Premises were opened not

Now changes became rapid and radical. Printing from metal, known as letterpress, was superseded by film, chemicals and plates or "offset-litho". The building was massively constructed and well able to bear the weight of several hundred tons of type metal and machinery. It was, however, of a multi-storey mill construction. In addition, traffic in Newcastle had multiplied to the extent that the town was frequently completely clogged with it. Sharing one narrow

Right: A hand fed Furnival litho press, printing from the original stone. The process has made huge strides since these early days, with the stones being replaced by thin aluminium sheets. **Top:** *A Linotype hot metal typesetting machine circa 1905.*

Left: The premises at High Bridge which the firm moved to in 1902.
Bottom left: John T Ward, Managing Director and the fourth generation of the Ward family to run the business.

Assembly Rooms. Six inches of snow ensured it was not the success it deserved to be but it has grown into one of the largest annual events of its kind in the country.

At the end of 1996 Wards took over Philipson & Son Ltd of Albany House. This company itself had a long history in Newcastle. In 1900 John Philipson bought a modest process engraving shop. It was gradually built up by his son James, becoming a limited company in 1923. In the thirties the photographic and artists' studios became a separate company. In

only in Percy Street but also in Hull, Carlisle, Middlesbrough and Sunderland. A factory shop was opened next to the printing works in Dunston which attracts considerable passing trade from people using the Metrocentre. In 1979 Ward's first exhibition promoting graphics was held in the old

the 50s and 60s expansion was renewed with the acquisition of Burrill & Co and of Hislop & Day Ltd. In 1970 Philipsons moved to Albany House. This is close to the centre of a massive regeneration scheme for the west end of the city, based on the millennium 'Centre for Life' project. A new Gallery and Art shop will shortly be opened, complementing the existing photographic, colour-separation and bureau complex.

The combined company has become a 'one-stop-shop' producing everything for visual and verbal communication. Organised into nine departments, including an interesting gallery and museum, its amalgamation of creative talents provides customers with a final graphics product at a competitive price on an agreed timescale.

Delivering only the freshest produce

To qualify for employment with Thomas Baty of Newcastle you would have to be willing to begin your working day at 3.30 am on six days a week. This is perhaps the one factor in the business that has not changed since the 1870s when it was first set up.

Its founder worked for another employer in the wholesale market for a while to learn the business of wholesaling fresh fruit and vegetables. When he felt confident enough to organise things himself he took premises in St Andrews Street and began trading. Flat barrows were pulled by porters and bigger loads transported in horse-drawn carts.

By the early 1900s his two sons, Alexander Thomas and William Henry were in their late teens and ready to join him in his business and the fourth generation of Batys are now in charge.

Batys ran their business from the same premises for just two years short of a century. Then the wholesale market was relocated to Gateshead away from the congestion of the city centre. Transport of supplies from growers and from the docks is never and has never been as quick as wholesalers would like. Also, some produce, especially fruit, is hard to source. Strangely, during the First World War, bananas procured for the miners were fairly easily available. The main suppliers are the UK and Europe. In the appropriate seasons fruit is bought from the Far East and the Americas.

The firm's main customers are green-grocers, caterers and take-away businesses, mostly local. The major super-markets have not obtained their fruit, vegetables and exotics from the wholesalers for more than twenty years and Baty's are anxious to help their customers compete against them. They pride themselves on delivering fresh produce direct from abroad or the UK grower.

Above: The founder, Thomas Baty. **Below:** *Thomas Baty's premises circa 1920.*

Turnbulls - taking pride in their service

In 1871 Edwin and Frederick Turnbull established a Company for the purchase and distribution of general household goods. For this purpose they took a warehouse in High Friar Street (which is now part of the Eldon Square complex). Business progressed steadily despite a move to temporary premises in Darn Crook, whilst repairs were carried out to the war damaged building. In the early sixties new premises were sought due to the compulsory purchase of the High Friar Street premises.

The business of R. Robinson & Sons had meanwhile grown to become one of the largest printers in the North of England and in 1898 had commissioned the architect Frank Rich to build them a new warehouse in Clavering Place, close to the High Level Bridge. This fine building served them well for many years but eventually that business ran into difficulties and the premises were acquired by E & F Turnbull Ltd. They adapted it to their own purposes and the business continues to the present day when it is now in its fifth generation.

The company's insistence on meticulous behaviour led to an amusing incident between the wars. The managing director of the day came downstairs and saw a boy sitting on the counter swinging his feet. The boy had been sent in by one of the market traders to collect a parcel. Thinking him to be one of his own staff idling his time, Mr Turnbull gave him ten shillings and told him to get away home and not come back! The boy collected his parcel and went on his way marvelling at his good fortune!

Over the years horse and cart has given way to a fleet of modern vehicles and E & F Turnbull's now deliver to shops and stores throughout Northern England and the whole of Scotland. They pride themselves on their choice of stock and their ability to give prompt and regular deliveries. The fine warehouse which is illustrated here serves them well and their offices which front onto Clavering Place were formerly the home of one of Newcastle's wealthy families when this part of town was a fashionable residential area. A number of scenes from the Catherine Cookson television dramas were filmed in these premises.

Above and below:
The same building a century apart.(the top picture shows the building only partially complete.)

The Bemco Story

The British Electrical and Manufacturing Company of Newcastle upon Tyne originated as The Tyneside Electrical Supply Company, which was founded in 1893. This latter Company was formed by Messrs Goolden and Pendlington to supply electrical equipment to industrial users in the North East of England and as a purchasing company for one of the first organisations in the world to cut coal by electricity, the Electrical Coal Cutting Contract Corporation.

In 1902, the original partners were joined by two brothers, Robert and Herbert Barkes, who introduced further capital. This was used to expand the business by opening new branches at Sunderland in 1905 and London in 1907 and by establishing a small manufacturing unit making switch and fusegear.

In 1908, the Company's name was changed to The British Electrical and Manufacturing Company, and in 1910 the Barkes brothers became the sole owners.

In the early years, BEMCO supplied a variety of electrical materials mainly to the Collieries, Shipyards, Steel Works and Railways. These included lamps and signalling equipment specially made to mining and railway requirements, black adhesive tape which was imported from America by the ton, knife switches, switchgear and cables of all types, including the first trailing cables used in the pits.

Top right: The Despatch Department. *Top left:* The cable section of warehouse number one. *Below:* Bemco's head office at Clavering Place, Newcastle, shortly after the company's move there in 1919.

Shortly after the outbreak of war in 1914, the manufacturing unit was sold due to a shortage of skilled labour, but in 1919 a further branch was opened in Glasgow and the main business moved from St. Nicholas' Buildings to the present site in Clavering Place.

Working conditions during the thirties were far different from those of today, pay was very low, and overtime was paid at a rate of 1/6d and the normal working week included Saturday mornings. Nobody started at the top, managers worked their way up from the bottom by being successful in all spheres of work for the company. Hard physical work was often the order of the day and many goods, including heavy, lead covered cables would be delivered by hand.

Even in the accounts department, everything was manual; invoices and ledgers were all hand written and everything was totalled mentally. In 1940, a Burroughs adding machine was a big innovation and in 1959-60 the accounts became mechanised on to accounting cards. It wasn't until 1970 that the firm went computerised and without this advance in technology, the staff wouldn't have been able to deal with the increased turnover.

Since 1945, branches have been opened at Abingdon, Edinburgh, Galashiels, Leeds and Wandsworth and the manufacturing works re-established in Glasgow. This unit designs and assembles specialist switch and distribution boards, mainly for the supply authorities in Scotland and the North of England, as well as building electrical control panels for industry.

BEMCO has been in the electrical supply and distribution business from almost the very start of the electrical era. It has grown, in fact, with electricity itself. Today, with its branches and manufacturing works, it is controlled by the sons, grandsons and nephews of the original founders.

Top: *One of the fancy fittings showrooms in the late twenties.*
Left: *The Main office.*

Thomas Owen - The story of the travelling saddler

The well-known Newcastle firm known as Thomas Owen and Sons Ltd. has been operating in the north east for almost a century and a half. The founding father who gave his name to the organisation was born in Shrewsbury, the son of a brewer. In his youth he trained as a saddler, and his ambition led him to leave his home town seeking fame and fortune as a travelling saddler, taking his brother Obadiah with him on the journey. Travelling saddlers would cover huge distances in those days, doing work on the farms they came across on an ad-hoc basis. The process was often referred to as "Whipping the Cat" - a term which was derived from the unwelcome attention received from the inhabitants of the various barns which the travelling craftsmen had to sleep in. Cats in particular became the travellers' pet aversion and so the term "Whipping the Cat" became adopted. The Owen brothers' travels took them to Stagshaw Fair in Northumberland. The brothers were typical of forward-thinking entrepreneurs of the Victorian Age. Thomas set up a saddlers shop in Bellingham in 1857. Early success due to his attention to detail and determination to succeed enabled Obadiah to open another shop in Corbridge. It was around this time that Thomas met his future wife, Susannah who was the schoolmistress in the village at the time.

The business grew steadily and the

brothers began selling cycle tyres as well as their saddlery products. Obadiah Owen's proud boast was that he was the first person to sell petrol in the Corbridge area, at the start of the 'transport revolution.'

Thomas Owen knew that significant additional growth could be achieved by gaining access to the market in nearby Newcastle. Consequently, in 1857, premises were acquired in the historic alleyway known as Dog

Above: Thomas Owen the company founder. Above right: A horse in harness from Thomas Owen's saddlers shop. Right: An early view of Side. Facing page, top: The Percy Street Shop. Facing page, bottom: Thomas Owen & Sons Ltd at 40-46 Side in the late 1950s.

the firm. Thomas and Susannah Owen had eight children, one son, Frank, and seven daughters. At the turn of the century one of their daughters, Nora, ran a wholesale toy business for Thomas Owen based in Handyside Arcade, Percy Street. Eventually she took this business over. Frank worked in the business until the First World War, when he joined the Forces as a Saddler in the Royal Naval Division. In the last days of the War Frank heard the sad news that his father was critically ill, and Frank was discharged on compassionate grounds on 10th November 1918. His father died the day after, Armistice Day 1918, leaving instructions that the business he had built was to be divided equally between his children, and control passed into the hands of executors for a period of ten years. Frank gained control of the business in 1922, though

Leap Stairs, in the shadow of the Castle, the traditional centre of Newcastle's leather trade. The business flourished and soon outgrew those early premises. Within a few years property at 77-83 Side was acquired to cope with the increasing number of customers attracted to

remains to this day. Throughout the history of the firm many diverse products have been offered. At the turn of the century galoshes were big sellers. These protective rubber shoe coverings kept out the worst of the mud and wet weather but are all but unheard of among today's younger generation. Other popular products included many items of saddlery for the coal mining industry which relied upon the work of pit-ponies, as well as saddlery used by industrial firms with teams of horses used for deliveries. Hot water bottles were another popular line, long before the days when most homes had central heating. Countless thousands of rubber boots have been sold by the company over the years throughout the north east of England. Waterproof clothing of all types was another important category of business, as was protective sheeting for the back of carts and lorries.

the dispute about ownership went on for many more years, and took a courageous decision which was to shape the nature of the firm for many years to come. The decline of the traditional saddlery trade was inevitable as a consequence of the rise of motor-powered transport but a saddlers shop was opened in 1928 in Percy Street, Newcastle. Frank decided to develop lines in industrial factoring - supplying a wide range of products used by industrialists throughout the region, a characteristic of the business which

Frank Owen met and later married Charlotte, a schoolmistress like his mother, and between them they had three children. Charlotte was born in 1916,

Thomas William in 1918 and Kenneth Atkinson who was born in 1921. Frank maintained an interest in the saddlery trade up until 1932. At this time a lease was acquired on a shop in Hexham and the organisation began selling various types of clothing for the first time. Thomas William Owen, at the age of 19, went to Walsall to learn about the saddlery trade in 1937. When he rejoined the business in Newcastle he also joined the Territorial Army and was called up shortly afterwards when the Second World War broke out. Kenneth, his brother, was articled as a Quantity Surveyor and also joined up. Thankfully both brothers returned safely from the war and Kenneth helped his mother on the clothing side of the firm. Some involvement with saddlery existed for a further 15 years but moves were made towards the supply of heavy canvass and tarpaulin during this time. Frank Owen died in 1972 at the age of 75. His son Thomas William later retired, and Kenneth's son Roger had already joined the business. The property located at 40-46 The Side in Newcastle had been built by Frank Owen, (over a period of eight years following the war) and the business had operated there for a period of 43 years. Eventually it was accepted that the company had outgrown the premises and it was decided to re-locate in a modern single-storey building with better parking and access for distribution purposes.

The company is now managed by the fifth generation of the Owen family, Roger, ably assisted by his wife Jennifer and their daughter Sarah who has recently joined the business. It is firmly established as a major supplier of cleaning and hygiene products, floor machines, safety footwear and clothing. Thomas Owen's premises can be found along the Fossway on

Brough Park Industrial Estate on the outskirts of Newcastle, staffed by a dedicated team of twenty, each equipped with a specialist knowledge of a particular field of the business. The company ethos considered the value of superior customer service as a priority long before this became fashionable in 'management' books and seminars. Indeed, present members of the Owen family believe that this tradition began with Thomas Owen himself, and has been 'the way things get done' in the organisation ever since. The firm is proud to remain essentially a family business and proud of its long history and association with the north east. But this does not mean that the directors at Thomas Owen are backward looking. They prefer to think of themselves as achieving an ideal blend of the virtues of the past with the technical and commercial advantages of the present day. This is a philosophy that Thomas Owen would have approved of, and one which has resulted in a growing number of loyal customers in Tyneside and beyond and as a result of this they have been finalists in the National Distributor of the Year Awards for the past three years.

*Above right: Kenneth Owen, left and Roger Owen, right, outside the new premises. **Left:** The staff based at the unit at Brough Park. **Facing page, top:** The original Hexham shop. **Facing page, bottom:** A member of staff finishing off a pair of rubber boots.*

The Grainger Trust - carving a niche in the property market

The Grainger Trust is a residential property investment company which was founded in 1912 by Robert Dickinson and Russell Storey. The former was a solicitor, senior partner in Dickinson Miller and Turnbull solicitors at Cross House, Newcastle (now Dickinson Dees, St. Ann's Wharf) and the latter an estate agent, a senior partner of what is now Storey Sons and Parker.

The new company conducted its business in Cross House where Mr Dickinson continued his practice, and the property investment concern stayed there until 1974.

Its activities consisted of property investment, management and letting. The bulk of the housing stock came from owners in such traditional industries as British Coal, British Steel and English China Clay. These companies sold their tenanted stock which the Trust bought and managed.

From the sixties it has also become involved in residential land development and the ownership of commercial properties.

In 1975 a move was made to a new headquarters at Royal Buildings. Later there was a further move to the present premises in Chaucer Buildings, 57 Grainger Street.

Business has continued steadily since 1912 with few problems. Like most businesses, they suffered inconveniences during the two World Wars. From 1939 to 1945 the company suffered property losses through bombing damage as well as the minor inconveniences caused by government restrictions.

Three generations of the Dickinson family have been involved in managing the company. Currently Robert Dickinson is Chairman and his cousin

> **"THE COMPANY'S ACTIVITIES CONSIST OF PROPERTY INVESTMENT, MANAGEMENT AND LETTING"**

Stephen is Managing Director. Another cousin, Rupert Dickinson is also a Director of the company. Mr Stephen Dickinson practised as an Chartered Accountant in the British Virgin Islands until he was called back to Britain to manage the Trust in 1974. The company became quoted on the London Stock Exchange in 1983.

Despite the housing recession of the nineties the company continues to flourish. It is already seeing some recovery in the south of England and looks forward to its spread through the Midlands to the North. It has been active in rationalising its commercial portfolio and the benefits of more intensive management are starting to show.

The Directors are confident of the Group's potential to pursue successfully niche opportunities in the property market, having already increased the market value of its trading stock.

The staff at Chaucer Buildings consider it not the least of their achievements that they have finally persuaded Northern Goldsmiths to get their clock to work!

Opposite page: The splendid Northern Goldsmiths building at the bottom of Northumberland Street, pictured at the turn of the century, which now belongs to the Grainger Trust Group.
This page top left: Robert Dickinson, Chairman of the Grainger Trust Group. Above: Stephen Dickinson, Managing Director.

The river of constant change

During the Roman period, the importance of the River Tyne was strategic as a supply line to the many forts along the Wall guarding its northern frontier.

Trade in later medieval times centred on the export of wool, hides, grindstones and lead with coal steadily increasing in importance from 1600 onwards.

The upsurge in trade and industry fuelled by the Industrial Revolution and an expanding railway network marked a growing need for improvements to the river.

Protest and clamour for change led to an Admiralty enquiry which largely upheld the complaints levelled at Newcastle by river users over many years, culminating in the River Tyne Improvement Act being passed by Parliament in 1850. The Act effectively ended Newcastle's ancient monopoly and provided for a sharing of the conservancy responsibilities of the river apportioned between Newcastle, Gateshead, Tynemouth, South Shields and the Admiralty.

The new River Tyne Commissioners immediately set about securing Parliamentary powers to build the two great masonry piers at the entrance to the river, alleviating the mariner's dread of the notorious Black Middens rocks and the Herd Sand. Thereafter quickly followed the commencement of dredging away the numerous shoals and sandbanks between Shields and Newcastle, deepening, straightening and widening the channel for the rapidly increasing number and size of ships using the river and encouraging the establishment of many docks, quays and shipyards. The river above Newcastle was similarly improved after 1876 when the old stone bridge was removed and replaced with the Swing Bridge.

The Tyne Improvement Commission controlled the river until superseded by the present Port Of Tyne Authority in 1968, worthy successors, who in their turn are no less ready to quickly respond to the changing trends and requirements of modern port conservancy.

After 1850 there was a rapid increase in ships using the river, particularly colliers loading and waiting to load coal. To provide more space to handle the increased traffic, Tyne Dock was created in 1859 and Northumberland Dock in 1867.

By 1872, work commenced on what was to become Albert Edward Dock within a large natural hollow on the north bank of the river downstream of

Top right: The final excavation to form the bottom of Albert Edward Dock was executed 'in the dry' with the entrance to the river sealed off. Left: Civic Dignatories and HRH Prince Albert on board the "Para e' Amazonas" for the official opening of the new dock in 1884.

Prince commented "lovely entrance, where's the dock?", which suggests that champagne was freely flowing on the passage from Newcastle Quay.

By the middle of the 19th century the growth in shipbuilding, engineering and coal exports from the river was enormous, with increasing need for river improvements.

Northumberland Dock called Coble Dene. Most of the 5,000,000 tons of material excavated was removed by dredgers and dumped at sea.

The official opening of the new dock in 1884 was a rather grand affair, with the principal guest being naturally Albert Edward Prince of Wales, who on his visit to the North East had already officiated at the opening of Jesmond Dene as a public park, the Hancock Natural History Museum and the new Public Library in Newcastle.

A colourful armada of vessels assembled at Newcastle Quay where the civic dignitaries of the day embarked for the procession down river. At their head steamed the new "Para e' Amazonas' with H.R.H. prominent on the upper deck. Rumour has it that the

In 1855 work commenced on the North and South Piers, a monumental task for Victorian engineers. There were many mishaps and set backs during the construction period due largely to the severity of north-easterly gales, which were a prominent feature of prevailing winter weather conditions on the east coast of Britain at that time. No less than four of the seven cranes on the North Pier and two of the four on the South Pier were torn from their mountings and washed into the sea during the winter of 1867 alone together with serious damage to the foundations of the completed portions of the Work. Similarly during the winter storms of 1893 and 1894 the large slewing cranes on both North and South Piers were lost.

Top: The severity of the weather conditions and force of the sea is amply illustrated in this picture recording the aftermath of the storms of 1897/98. The seas have undermined the foundation courses causing large sections to overbalance and topple, in addition to which, a complete breach of 300 feet had opened up. **Left:** Passenger ships of the Bergen Line and Olsen Line can be seen lying alongside dressed with bunting for the opening of the Tyne Commission Quay in 1928. A newly arrived passenger train is drawn up alongside the new terminal shed.

Realignment and reconstruction of the damage caused by the severe storms 1897/98 to the North Pier was not completed until 1909 - some fifty four years after commencement of the work at a total cost of £1,018,000. The South Pier too had mishaps, perhaps on a lesser scale, and was completed in 1895 at a cost of £450,000.

The intervening years between the two World Wars were marked by a steady increase in passenger traffic from the River Tyne, particularly to Scandinavia.

The need for a deep water quay to replace the outmoded passenger facility within Albert Edward

Work on the 335 metre concrete quay with 7.1 metre depth of water at low water was completed in 1928.

In 1936 coal still revailed as the major commodity in the region. On the 28th July a newly constructed timber shipping staith with overhead conveyors was officially opened by the Duke and Duchess of York, shortly to succeed to the throne on 12th December as King George VI and Queen Elizabeth following the abdication of Edward VI1. In 1985 Elizabeth, now Queen Mother, made a return visit to the river to open the brand new Tyne Coal Terminal at Tyne Dock, symbolically using the same electric switch which had activated the coal conveyors at Jarrow forty nine years earlier.

Like all the other docks, Tyne Dock was laid out as a railway dock from its inception in 1859. Dock roads were therefore minimal, with major imports of pit props, and sawn timber in huge quantities crane handled and transported from the ships in rail wagons to the various timber yards.

Dock was fulfilled by the construction of Tyne Commission Quay on the riverward side of the Dock in 1928 greatly improving ship turn round times and improving cargo handling facilities, with a rail link direct to the main line station at Newcastle.

Above: The Duchess of York unveiling a commemorative plaque set in the wall of the control building at the opening of the Jarrow Staithe in 1936. She is pictured with the Duke and Sir Arthur Sutherland, Chairman of the Tyne Improvement Commission. Top left: Another picture taken of the Jarrow Staithe opening from the opposite side of the river. The first vessel to be loaded can be seen alongside the coal conveyors bedecked with flags for the occasion. Left: An aerial view of Tyne Dock, 1951.

Within the dock, loading staiths were still exporting large quantities of coal to overseas markets at this point in time.

By 1951 preparatory work was already under way in the construction of the iron-ore import handling plant and associated concrete quay, and was completed and operational by 1953.

Since 1951 river associated commercial activity has gradually moved down river for economic reasons not the least being deeper water, closeness to the sea and the prohibitive cost- of dredging.

By 1974, with the exception of the quay, which was re-named Riverside Quay and now handles general cargo, all would be swept away in the gradual transformation of the dock facilities from rail to road transport. A new road complex and large modem transit sheds to accommodate mechanical cargo handling methods including containerisation all featured prominently in the modernisation.

The cranes and warehouses which once lined both sides of the river at Newcastle and Gateshead have been swept away, with promenades, lively bars and restaurants taking their place, earning Newcastle a national reputation for leisure and lively nightlife and bringing new life to an area slowly falling derelict.

Above: The hopper barge "Bobby Shaftoe" inward bound from sea in 1959, returning to berth at Stella Power Station after dumping her cargo of fly ash. Ahead can be seen the Tyne Bridge, High Level Bridge, Swing Bridge and in the far distance the King Edward Bridge. Left: The winter of 1962/63 in North Eastern England was unusually severe with arctic temperatures prevailing well into Spring. The enclosed Albert Edward and Tyne Docks, froze over, as did large stretches of the river itself above the tidal reaches. When the thaw eventually set in, the flow of broken slabs of ice passing through the channels of the Swing Bridge was more reminiscent of the St. Lawrence than the Tyne! This picture was taken from the control tower of the Swing Bridge looking down river towards Hillgate Quay on the Gateshead side of the river.

Just Ask

The key to our service' says a recent advertisement for North British Tapes Limited 'is Just Ask.'

The company doing the answering was originally named after its founders, Adolph and Sidney Albrecht. Entrepreneurs, starting from London, these two brothers set up in business to supply brakes and allied equipment for the trams in Gateshead and Newcastle.

The Company was the first tenant of Milburn House, renting basement offices and a workshop on the corner of Dean Street and the Side.

To prove that there is no such thing as a new idea, the premises even incorporated a gymnasium and shower for regular workouts by the staff - upstaging Japanese practices and the keep fit boom by a number of decades.

NORTH BRITISH ENGINEERING EQUIPMENT CO.
LIMITED

ELECTRICAL & MECHANICAL PLANT SUPPLIES

MILBURN HOUSE
NEWCASTLE UPON TYNE NE1 1NU

TELEPHONE: NEWCASTLE 25252 (PRIVATE EXCHANGE)

DIRECTORS
S. W. ALBRECHT
R. H. BRIDGES
M. D. REDFERN
H. G. BRIDGES

Important agency business for Albrechts in those early days was the Brill Track Company and Peacock Track Company.

In 1914, because of the impending war, Adolph, who was actually of Dutch descent, decided to change the company name to North British Engineering Equipment to overcome the possible prejudice of a German-sounding name. Records from this time show that the company's turnover for March was £75 15s 0d. The managing director in 1914 received £3 a week and the total wage bill was £18 12s, with one worker picking up commission for £1 11s 8d. There were obviously no such things as company cars, so the total bill for travel, by tram and other public transport, was £11 10s 0d.

After the Second World War the company had also taken on the agencies for Jackson cookers and Thor washing machines. In 1921, North British Engineering Equipment took on the agency for Ericsson Telephones for use in the NE coal mines. Such is the impact that the company made in that area, that, even at the end of the eighties, it was still receiving, albeit rarely, calls for replacement parts - even thought the agency was terminated in 1969 when the telephone company became part of Plessey.

"THE PREMISES EVEN INCORPORATED A GYMNASIUM AND SHOWER FOR REGULAR WORKOUTS BY THE STAFF"

However, in most other respects the inter war years were of mixed fortunes. Adolph returned to spend more time at his home in London. He was then the full time paid secretary of the Electrical Wholesalers' Federation and the running of the Newcastle business was taken over by his brother Sidney.

By this time the company had gradually moved into wholesaling of electrical equipment and was to continue such lines until the early sixties. By then, voracious acquisition by large nationals meant that a small company could not compete.

Above: A company letterhead from the days of the North British Enginering Equipment Company.
Facing page top: The company founder Adolf Albrecht.
Facing page bottom: An early view of The Side, Newcastle, where Adolf Albrecht's first premises were.

North British Engineering Equipment soon realised the potential for self adhesive tapes and began promoting transparent Scotch cellulose tape. It was becoming apparent that this was gradually superceding string in industry and commerce. By the eighties Scotch tapes were being used in batch production, having replaced traditional jointing methods such as screws and rivets.

Mike Bridges, the present managing director, joined the company in 1966 as a general dogsbody. He arrived fresh from graduating in English at St Andrews and was set to travelling round the NE, looking for business. Thanks partly to his efforts, the demand for tapes grew so that he was renting space from

In the late fifties the association began with 3M which was then known as the Minnesota Mining and Manufacturing Company. North British Engineering Equipment, as electrical wholesalers, had stocked that company's electrical insulating tape which had replaced the well known 'Blacklie' tape. The Minnesota company also produced magnetic recording tape, in spools rather than cassettes.

*Above: Mike Bridges and his Aunt, Miss Sydney Albrecht. **Below**: The original premises on Camperdown Industrial Estate. **Facing page top**: Mike Bridges looking to the future on the construction site of the new premises at Killingworth. **Facing page bottom**: An old advertisement for North British Tapes.*

Tapes also marketed their safety respirators, adhesives, abrasives and electrical products.

Here, in 1978, Mike Bridges succeeded his father Gerald as managing director, making a third generation of family management. The names Albrecht and Bridges were and are synonymous with North British Tapes and Miss Sydney Albrecht was the company accountant at Killingworth.

North British Engineering. He has since been joined in the company by his son, Toby, the fourth generation of the family to be involved inthe business.

In 1976 the company changed its name and North British Tapes emerged. In another two years the space at Milburn House had become too cramped and a move was made to a factory and office unit on the Camperdown Industrial Estate, Killingworth.

> **"THE COMPANY BELIEVES THAT THE VALUE OF ITS EXPANSIVE PRODUCT RANGE IS INCREASED BY ITS ATTENTION TO CUSTOMER SERVICE"**

1986 brought a distributorship agreement signed between North British Tapes Limited and 3M Telcomm Products Group whereby enquiries for Telcomm products were to be handled by North British Tapes' trained office staff or their team of technical representatives who would visit customers to discuss specific requirements on their premises.

Today, from its two centres in Killingworth, Newcastle upon Tyne and Hailes Park Industrial Estate, Edinburgh, North British Tapes is one of the UK's largest distributors of self adhesive tapes, abrasives, maintenance and electrical products.

The company believes that the value of its expansive product range is increased by its attention

Here, to begin with, the company employed 15 people. The association with 3M went from strength to strength. As well as their complete and diverse range of tape products, North British

North British Tapes Limited

Building for the future in North Tyneside

NORTH BRITISH TAPES

For more information on how we can facilitate your buying process in the production, packaging, electrical or maintenance department, just give us a call.

Newcastle
0191 268 6272

Edinburgh
0131 444 2226

"The Key To Our Service is Just Ask"

INVESTOR IN PEOPLE

surroundings and in the out-of-work-hours lives of its employees. It has offered, for example, financial and technical support to the Whitley Warriors Ice Hockey team and became the first adopter in the National Rivers Authority 'Adopt a Holt Scheme' to protect otters. This unique sponsorship scheme began during the National Otter Weekend in October 1993 when Bill Oddie and Colin Blundel from the NRA joined Mike Bridges, MD of North British Tapes at a secret (for obvious reasons) location, building the first holt in a limited adoption.

to customer service. When handling all queries, technical or otherwise, it is the company's aim to provide customers with a service second to none. Approved by BVQI, it has been awarded EN 29002, ISO 9002 and BS 5750.

The company takes a lively interest in its

Right: The first issue of the company's own newspaper. Above: Just a very small selection of the products available at North British Tapes, clockwise from top left; Pallet wrap film; Printed Tapes, these are printed in-house to suit all requirements; General Purpose Tapes; Hot Melt Adhesive for use on a variety of packaging applications; and Self Adhesive Packaging Tapes.

After 90 successful years in business, the firm has changed its trading style to "NBT" who will specialise in all adhesives and tapes and "TEKNORSOL" who will look after the electrical business. The company has now turned full circle from the early years at Milburn House when the Albrechts set up their business supplying electrical and mechanical products in 1908.

The outward-looking attitude is reflected in the company employee's mission statement, "Smiling and brimful of new ideas, we are enthusiastic and positive yet flexible. The quality of life at work, matched only by that outside, allows us to attain total fulfilment through our soaring reputation. Customers are delighted with the priceless service of a world class organisation and other firms seek our advice on how to run their companies. Who knows our limits?."

Above: From left to right, Mike Bridges, Colin Blundell from the National Rivers Authority and Bill Oddie, when the company became the first to adopt an otter holt during the National Otter Weekend in 1993.
Top right: *The new company logos.*
Below: *The new premises at Killingworth.*

John Porter (Newcastle) Ltd - the door set people

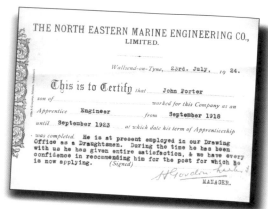

John Porter (Newcastle) Ltd. is a long established, privately owned firm of specialist joinery manufacturers. Its founder began his working life at the end of the First World War as an apprentice engineer at the North Eastern Marine Engineering Company Ltd, in Wallsend. After he completed his apprenticeship he became a journeyman draughtsman for the same company and later became personal assistant to the works manager.

In the late twenties his desire to see the world led him to take a job as a site engineer in Persia with the Anglo-Persian Oil Company, a forerunner of BP, where he was paid £740 a year, quite a sum for a young man in those days. As a result of desert living under canvas and despite keeping a string of polo ponies he was able to save a considerable amount of capital by 1931 and returned home.

He wanted to get away from the dirt and oil of engineering by this time and in 1932, with the help of several friends in the timber trade, started a woodworking business with a starting capital of £1000. The business started in a small factory in Bank Road, Gateshead and with his partner Bob Dixon, a technical expert, business grew steadily in a modest way. In 1933 John married Ruby Christie from Belfast who had been living in Earsdon with her brothers, Bert and Raymond, both practising GPs. In 1936 their son Brian was born and eventually he became the second generation to join the Company.

Also by 1936 more production space was required and a move was made to the present premises at St. Lawrence Road, Byker. This building was built in 1913 for Smith Ropery (Ropeworks) by Mouchel & Partners and was amongst the earliest buildings to be constructed in reinforced concrete in Newcastle for it retains many traditional timber construction details in the concrete. Its predecessors were the Co-op warehouse on the Quayside, now turned into a high class hotel, and Manors Goods Yard, since demolished to make way for the Warner cinema.

When war came John Porter, as a Lieutenant in the Royal Northumberland Fusiliers T. A., was posted off to active service and Bob Dixon kept the business going, manufacturing ammunition boxes amongst other war requirements. Work on Ouston airfield and for the shipyards meant employing a workforce of over 100 men.

After the war, despite the difficulties of continued timber control and rationing, a great deal of business came from housing contracts for developers such as William Leech and George Wimpey. The timber industry was still very traditional and supplies were obtained mostly locally from importers on the river such as Denny Mott & Dickson, Thompson Eyres & Clunie and M.H. Southern & Son Ltd who in those days were still on Skinnerburn Road before their move to Jarrow. They also dealt with Wm. Bell who had a sawmill behind the Central Station goods yard, now demolished to make way for the new Life Centre being built. This sawmill was run by Wylam Bell, a great chum of John Porter and an immense character in Northumberland golf circles before and after the war. At the start of the war he was in the army under canvas near Alnwick and was in the habit of going for a bath at the White Swan Hotel. One evening when he called he was given a clean towel by the receptionist before going upstairs. A visiting Brigadier General spotted this and also asked for a bath. "I'm sorry sir" said the receptionist "There are no baths tonight - because of the War".

"But I saw that Corporal going for a bath" said the General.

Above: John Porter's apprenticeship certificate.
Top left: John Porter in his Lieutentant's uniform.
Left: The workshop interior.

"That was no Corporal, sir" replied the receptionist "That was Mr Bell".

In the fifties and sixties freighters of Ellerman, Bibby, Palm Line and others used to unload huge hardwood logs onto the quay below the John Porter factory; utile, iroko and sapele from Africa with meranti and teak from the Far East. These were mostly destined for the Tyne Plywood factory but they were amongst the most difficult and dangerous bulk cargoes to unload.

Deep sea ships no longer dock in Newcastle but all of these timbers are still used in the manufacture of joinery, although now much less so than northern hemisphere hardwoods from more carefully managed sources in Europe and North America.

One of the last contracts which John Porter himself obtained was the supply of all the joinery for Newcastle's new Civic Centre. It was a special pleasure to work with Sir Robert McAlpine on this project as it was one of the few buildings at that time to be built up to a standard and not down to a price.

Other contracts remembered with pride are the Newcastle Airport, Durham's County Hall at Ayckley Heads, the Main Building at DHSS Longbenton and the physics building at Newcastle University by Sir Basil Spence. The founder's son Brian, who had qualified as a chartered accountant after National Service in the Royal Navy, joined the business in 1962 and now the third generation of Porters works in the business as his son Timothy was appointed Production Director in 1997.

As the housing boom subsided, John Porter Ltd. developed an expertise in the production of fire resistant timber doors and doorsets. They were commissioned by the D.H.S.S. to develop a whole range of doorsets for hospital buildings and were one of only five firms approved by the PSA to supply Government contracts. Their doors are now to be found in the royal kitchens of Buckingham Palace, the London Hospital, St. Bartholomews and many other hospitals locally and throughout the country. They have supplied doors from North Unst, Shetland to the Falkland Islands and to Poland and Uganda. Their range of specialist doors includes acoustic doors, security and x-ray proof doors faced with any desired material.

Until the last decade the technology of woodworking machinery had not really changed much since the Company was founded but the fine tolerances now demanded for fire and smoke resistant doorsets can only be met by increased use of computer controlled machinery. Nevertheless, many of the old hand craftsman's operations continue. The traditions of skilled craftsmen continue in the Company which last year had a wood machinist retire after 50 years service with the Company. There is a growing demand for quality doors and frames with proven performance and the Company know that its reputation in this field continues to grow. This is a Company where production is 'up to standard and not down to a price'.

Top right: The Civic Centre Rates Hall.
Left: Craft Work.
Below: The company premises.

The story of good Manners

Northumberland was one of the main fat stock producing counties. Its heavy land pastures have been made productive when early work at the Cockle Park Research Station affirmed the value of basic slag for improving grassland.

The Manners family of five brothers farmed along this great belt of fattening country which covered 4,000 acres.

R Manners & Sons was first established over 80 years ago. That was when the grandfather of the current directors, Ian and Geoffrey Manners, decided that, with six children, it was easier to procure meat from his own livestock than to buy it.

Soon, Robert had begun a business by selling any surplus meat, running a small farm and butcher's shop near Bishop Auckland. His son, Jim (Ian, the current Chairman's father) preferred farming to butchering and Northumberland to Durham.

With his wife and his son Jim, Robert came to High Weetslade, Dudley and began farming there.

Right: The founder, Robert Manners. **Below:** *The shop at Coundon, near Bishop Auckland , 1913.*

firm had contracts to supply hospitals, schools, canteens and industrial concerns.

As well as working to excellent effect together, the brothers worked on their own initiative. Jim Manners, whose farm was at Preston Mains, Chathill, expanded his market by developing a bakery to supply hot meat pies through his own shops.

In addition he took a substantial interest in a new steak bar in Newcastle, known as 'Jim's Inn'. Being in a position to obtain the very best, this establishment built up a wide clientele on recommendation of satisfied clients.

His family grew to five sons and two daughters and, during the thirties the family launched themselves back into butchering. Both branches of the business grew side by side. The shop opened in Newcastle was the first of a string, eventually totalling eight branches. Meanwhile, the sons of the family left home to farm on their own account.

THE FARM SHOP
WEST MOOR, FOREST HALL
Telephone 61134

R. Manners & Sons

239
CHILLINGHAM RD
HEATON
Telephone 56220

FAMILY BUTCHERS

ALL MEAT, EGGS & POULTRY DIRECT FROM OUR OWN FARM
SPECIAL QUOTATIONS TO HOTELS AND INSTITUTES

Hector Manners originally was in milk production but found it more profitable to follow the family trend into beef production.

When the site of the West House slaughterhouse was taken over in the development of the new town at Killingworth, Mr George Manners was given just five weeks to clear the land. Tired of waiting for Newcastle City to provide adequate

A small amount of slaughtering went on at High Weetslade, the farm where they lived. The family later acquired the farm at West House and set up a slaughtering facility where animals from the five Manners farms were killed before being sent to the family shops.

War and rationing put a temporary stop to the development but, once restrictions were relaxed the business expanded and the shops were soon supplying meat to people all over Tyneside. In addition the

Top: West Moor Shop, Newcastle circa 1930. Centre: An early invoice. Right: Meat preparation at Ponteland in 1964.

facilities the Manners brothers decided to go ahead on their own. Jim Manners travelled extensively, searching for a design that would cope not only with the demand for their own shops but which could also handle meat for other butchers in the area.

Eventually, in 1964, the Manners family established the abattoir at Ponteland and it was officially opened by the Duke of Northumberland. Its attractive buildings gave little indication of their purpose but it provided unrivalled facilities in the area. It was ideally situated next to the Ponteland Auction Mart. It had the most modern equipment and the most hygienic conditions. There was a resident meat inspector and the premises could handle over 100 cattle at one time, all under cover.

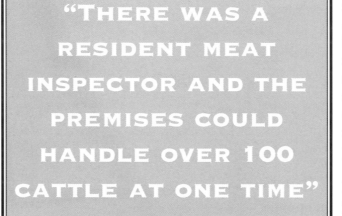

"THERE WAS A RESIDENT MEAT INSPECTOR AND THE PREMISES COULD HANDLE OVER 100 CATTLE AT ONE TIME"

The Manners brothers sent 150-200 cattle through the abattoir every week, only venturing into the open market when demand from the shops required it. The same high standards as for cattle were extended to sheep.

Jim Manners was a member of the Alnwick branch of the NFU for 21 years, sometimes their chairman and a delegate to the executive. In 1965 he

was made a Freeman of the City of London and later became a member of the Worshipful Company of Butchers of the City of London, a great honour for a butcher from the provinces.

In the nineties, still based in Ponteland, R Manners & Sons Ltd is being run by the third generation from its founder. It supplies a wide variety of customers with a broad spectrum of fresh and frozen meat and poultry products.

Ingenious systems in the present factory make it as simple as possible to run and scrupulously hygienic. For example, all lighting is controlled by sensors so that no-one has to touch a light switch. Manners is the chosen supplier for an ever-increasing number of catering outlets including nine local authorities, many

Top: The abattoir at Ponteland in 1964.
Right: The Pork Shop on Chillingham Road, Newcastle.

Borders to North Yorkshire and over to Cumbria.

factory canteens, hospitals, hotel chains, and various pubs, restaurants and nursing homes. The company insists on meat being procured only from approved and audited establishments but, even so, all processes are subject to its own fully trained quality control inspectors.

Within the plant, process machinery is set out logically with meat moving constantly in one direction. Discarded packaging meanwhile moves in another thus reducing the risk of cross-contamination during further processing. Regular, systematic inspections are undertaken by EEC veterinary personnel ensuring that their own controls are adhered to throughout processing.

There are two metal detecting systems in operation in the factory. One is on-line in the sausage production area and the other is at the end of the conveyor packing line which includes a modern, computerised digital weighing system. This last can relay individual customer specifications to the highly skilled butchers as each order is being processed, weighed, labelled and metal-detected before being dispatched.

The orders are delivered in a fleet of 16 dual-compartment, temperature controlled vehicles which cover an area from the Scottish

Manners form part of the 'National Catering Butcher Limited', a group of companies all NACB approved which together serve the UK. Every vehicle has radio contact with head office , making complete flexibility possible whilst they are on the road.

In an industry that has seen more than its fair share of troubles over the past few years, it is becoming increasingly uncommon to find a company which is both optimistic and excited about the future. However, the future looks bright indeed for this north eastern market leader.

Top left: An aerial view of Manners Meats as it appears today. ***Top right:*** *Ian Manners, Chairman of R. Manners Ltd.* ***Below:*** *The late Duke of Northumberland and the late Jim Manners, father of the current Chairman, at the opening of the Ponteland Abattoir in 1964.*

The customer first, next and always

Thomas Potter (Newcastle) Ltd, currently the largest independent distributor of industrial fastenings, flanges and tube in the North East, began its existence in December 1923. This was when Mr Thomas Potter entered into partnership with Mr Alf Wilkinson. Some time later the latter gentleman acquired the majority shares. They were stockists and distributors of fastenings, flanges and tools and their address was Stowell Street in Newcastle. A brisk trade was done in rivets for ship-building especially during the two wars.

After serving in the Royal Air Force as a pilot, Mr Norman Lister, Mr Wilkinson's nephew, returned to become managing Director. He had previously worked for his uncle in the firm's warehouse. His son, Mr Tony Lister came to work for the company in 1972. Beginning in the warehouse as his father had before him he worked in every department, becoming Sales Director in 1986. When Norman Lister retired his son succeeded him as Managing Director.

The firm had moved from Stowell Street to Market Street in 1930 where it remained until

shipbuilding and ship repairing companies as well as the engineering and the building and construction industry. Customers include large public limited companies and household names and are renowned for their large stockholding and their quick and efficient service. The current turnover is in excess of £4.6 million. They are therefore in a good position to fulfil their future plan to open further branches in other regions.

1967. In 1968 the company was bought by a Birmingham based concern which provided the finance to move to a new modern premises at Industry Road.

In December 1996 Mr Tony Lister, with the backing of 3i and Barclay's Bank, successfully acquired the entire share capital of the company in the form of a management buy-out. He has opened branches at Aycliffe, Middlesbrough and Sunderland and a manufacturing company, 'Potter Engineering' at Fisher Street, Walker. They still supply

Maybe the secret of their success is a placard on display in the company's

tp WHAT IS A CUSTOMER ? **tp**

A Customer is the MOST IMPORTANT PERSON IN THIS BUSINESS, in person, by letter or by telephone.
A Customer is not dependent on us but WE ARE DEPENDENT ON HIM, WITHOUT HIM WE CLOSE DOWN.
A Customer is NOT AN INTERRUPTION OF OUR WORK – HE IS THE PURPOSE OF IT.
A Customer is not someone to match wits with, or argue with, as NO ONE EVER WON AN ARGUMENT WITH A CUSTOMER.
A Customer is a person who brings us his wants. It is our business to handle his wants profitably to HIM AND TO US. We should see that nothing is left undone either in attention, workmanship or materials to ensure his complete satisfaction. THAT IS WHY WE ARE IN BUSINESS.
This is what a Customer is, in this business or any other business so it is up to us to see THAT WE GET AND KEEP SATISFIED CUSTOMERS – and to spare no effort in doing this.
When dealing with Customers then, directly or i directly, keep this before you and realise that HE IS THE BUSINESS FIRST, SECOND AND ALWAYS.

THOMAS POTTER (NEWCASTLE) LIMITED

workplaces. Headed, "What is a customer?" the staff are reminded that he is someone they are dependent upon, that he is not an interruption of their work but the reason for it, that he is not someone to argue with, that, in short, he is the reason why the company is in business.

*Facing page top right: Market Street with Manors in the background. **Bottom:** Croft House, on Market Street. **This page top left:** Friars House, on Stowell Street, home to Thomas Potter until the move to Market Street in 1930. **Top right:** Another view of Market Street. **Bottom left:** The premises on Industry Road, Heaton with W.D. and H.O. Wills building to the rear. **Above:** The placard displayed in the company's workplaces, stating the reason why the company is in business.*

The college with a great deal to offer

Newcastle College is a direct descendant of Rutherford College, founded about a hundred years ago in Bath Lane.

John Hunter Rutherford was an evangelical preacher who built on the site first a church, then a school, then a School of Science and Art, all in Corporation Street. When the accommodation became too small the city council made land available in Bath Lane for a new college. This was opened by the future King George V in 1894.

Soon this building too was too small for the numbers of students who enrolled. By 1907 the City Council had taken over as Dr Rutherford had died some years earlier. They added a new technical wing, the foundation stone of which was laid by the famous explorer, Sir Ernest Shackleton in 1909. The two-storey building was opened in 1910 and a third storey was added during the First World War. The Technical College remained here until 1956.

It continued to grow throughout that period. To cope, evening classes were initiated and, with the post-second-war emphasis on technical education, plans for a new college were discussed. The Newcastle education authority, however, was not impressed and made no move to improve conditions so that London University withdrew its recognition of the college's courses.

Things looked up when the buildings became the College of Further Education in 1956. There were further improvements when it became the basis of the Charles Trevelyan Technical College in 1964 but the bulky technical equipment needed to teach engineering and even greater numbers of students meant that, yet again, accommodation was soon inadequate.

In line with the Industrial Training Act of 1964 integrated education was developed and training courses were set up in engineering craft, electrical installation, radio and television and the building and timber trades. Student numbers continued to grow .

In 1966 a new Department of General Studies was introduced, though the college remained wedded to technical education. As the establishment of the Polytechnic became imminent, HNC courses were transferred to the college.

The College of Further Education, established in 1964, lasted until 1972 when it was formally amalgamated with the Charles Trevelyan Technical College to form the College of Arts and Technology. Its main work was the provision of courses for apprentices and technicians.

The present Newcastle College was established towards the end of 1988. The simple name brought it in line with Newcastle University and Newcastle Polytechnic. Under the provisions of the Education Reform Act the college began to ease away

through to degree level students, and covering areas such as art and design, performing arts, engineering and construction, hairdressing, travel and tourism, business and management and of course Information Technology. And today there's far greater flexibility for learning so that not only school leavers but also adults of all ages can learn at times and places to suit them; classes run during

from local authority control. The college welcomed its 'freedom to manage' whilst regretting the breaking of ties which had been amicable. The final break came with incorporation in 1993.

Millions of pounds have been invested to create a pleasant and convenient study environment. The college has three libraries and all students have access to the best IT facilities. The main campus has a sports centre, refectories and coffee bars, a gallery which exhibits students' art work, shops and hairdressing and beauty salons. All kinds of support are offered, including course advice, accommodation, welfare and financial advice and the services of the college chaplain. There are literally hundreds of courses, catering for absolute beginners

the day, in the evenings and at weekends, and there are new campuses at Hexham and Cramlington, taking education to the students rather than expecting them to travel to the city.

*Facing page top: The Parsons Building under construction in 1973. **Bottom:** Early college prospectuses from 1959 and 1961. **This page top:** Rock icon Sting took time out of a busy tour to give music students a masterclass in 1997. **Below right:** The Rye Hill Campus as it appears today. **Below:** Rob Andrews, Newcastle Falcons' Director of Rugby, opens the college media centre in 1998.*

Eldon Square - shopping that stretches the imagination

The site of the Eldon Square Shopping Centre is irregular and covers about ten acres in the shape of a letter F. It is in the heart of the central area of Newcastle and had to be developed in accordance with the framework established by the City Planning Department.

Because of the size and complexity of the development the shopping centre was built in two phases, both opening in 1976. The first consisted of 17 shops, three of which, Habitat, Mothercare and WH Smith, were new to the city. Six months later, in September, Phase 2 followed and included two new stores, Boots and Bainbridge.

November of the same year saw the opening of Eldon Square Recreation Centre, the largest indoor recreation centre incorporated in a shopping

complex in Europe. The entertainment use is over the shopping in the south block and runs the entire length of Blackett Street. The accommodation consists of two multi-purpose sports halls, an indoor bowling green, squash courts, judo, sauna, restaurant and bars.

The Centre was extended in 1987 when it covered 10 acres of Newcastle city centre. It is owned on a partnership basis of 40% by the city of Newcastle, 30%

Above and left: Some of Eldon Square's high quality retail outlets which attract shoppers from all over the area.

week, peaking to 700,000 in December. 30% of shoppers visit on a Saturday and, surprisingly, only 27% visit by car.

Two customer service desks give a variety of information and sell souvenirs. In Spring 1997 the Eldon Square Loyalty Card was introduced. There is an in-Centre wheelchair service, cashpoints, dry cleaning, shoe repair and post office facilities. Mall security officers, helped by an efficient CCTV system covering all areas of the Centre ensure the safety and comfort of all customers.

Whatever advantages the individual store can offer, Eldon Square has moulded these together so that the benefits of the whole are greater than the sum of its parts. This is partly due to the way the shop fronts are open to the malls. This style has been much copied since its inception in Eldon Square.

by Shell Pension Trust and 30% by Capital Shopping Centres PLC.

Eldon Square provides employment for a total of 6,000 people. Trade flourishes at the centre and the satisfaction of the retailers is reflected in a unit turnover of less than 3% a year. Shoppers are brought in on bus trips from Weardale, Cumbria, Teesside and the Borders.

Eldon Centre has continued to grow in spite of improved shopping facilities in the rest of the surrounding area. The biggest threat was posed by the Metro Centre which, when it first opened in 1987, reduced the numbers using Eldon Square by 10%. However, trade was back to its original level within two years and it has continued to grow. Presently Eldon Square averages 473,000 visitors a

Capital Shopping Centres PLC was formed in March 1994 and comprised seven major shopping centres. Eldon Square was included, together with centres in Nottingham, Wakefield, the Potteries and three centres on the M25. In 1995 the Metro Centre of Gateshead was acquired.

Above: Eldon Square can be reached by train from British Rail Central Station.
Top: The attractive entrance to the shopping centre.
Left: A warm welcome in light and open malls, a style much copied since its introduction in the Eldon Square Shopping Centre.

Children from the West End of Newcastle 'mucking in' to prepare their street for the festivities celebrating the coronation of Queen Elizabeth in June 1953

First published in Great Britain by True North Holdings
Dean Clough
Halifax
West Yorkshire HX3 5AX
1998

All rights reserved. No part of this publication may be reproduced, stored in a retrieval system, or transmitted in any form, or by any means, electronic, mechanical, photocopy, recording or otherwise without the prior permission in writing of the Copyright holders (i.e True North Holdings), nor be otherwise circulated in any form or binding or cover other than in which it is published and without a similar condition being imposed on the subsequent publisher.

PHOTOGRAPH COMPILATION/DESIGN...MARK SMITH
CAPTIONS RESEARCH AND COMPILATION.......................................PHIL HOLLAND
DESIGNERS...MANDY WALKER & NICKY BRIGHTON
COPYWRITER...PAULINE BELL
BUSINESS DEVELOPMENT EDITOR..GARETH MARTIN

© TRUE NORTH HOLDINGS
ISBN 1 900 463 81 4